A
Führer
for a Father

JIM DAVIDSON is an historian, biographer and former editor of *Meanjin* (1975–82). He has been an academic and an opera critic, and is the author of two prize-winning biographies: *Lyrebird Rising: Louise Hanson-Dyer of Oiseau-Lyre, 1884–1962* (1994), and *A Three-Cornered Life: The Historian WK Hancock* (2010), which won the Prime Minister's Prize for Australian History, a Western Australian Premier's Award, and the *Age* Book of the Year for non-fiction. Jim is also the co-author of *Holiday Business: Tourism in Australia since 1870* (2000); his most recent book is *Moments in Time: A book of Australian postcards* (2016). He is a Baillieu Library Fellow at the University of Melbourne. In 2012 he was appointed AM, for a life of exemplary irregularity.

A Führer for a Father

The domestic face of colonialism

Ian
A receipt for the 2014
RGM Fellowship!
All best   Jim

JIM DAVIDSON

NEWSOUTH

A NewSouth book

Published by
NewSouth Publishing
University of New South Wales Press Ltd
University of New South Wales
Sydney NSW 2052
AUSTRALIA
newsouthpublishing.com

National Library of Australia
Cataloguing-in-Publication entry
Creator: Davidson, Jim, 1942–, author.

Title: A Führer for a Father: the domestic face of colonialism / Jim Davidson.
ISBN: 9781742235462 (paperback)
      9781742242811 (ebook)
      9781742248295 (ePDF)
Subjects: Davidson, Jim, 1942–
  Davidson, Jim, 1942 – Childhood and youth.
  Authors – Biography.
  Gay men – Australia – Biography.
  Fathers and sons – Australia – Biography.

Design Josephine Pajor-Markus
Cover design Blue Cork
Front cover image Olga and her keeper, Melbourne Zoo, c. 1942, courtesy of the
author. *Back cover images* Father in Papua, with Uau, c. 1936, courtesy of the
National Archives of Australia; Author aged fourteen, courtesy of the author.
Printer Griffin Press

Contents

Preface — vii

I   A frontiersman marries — 1

II   A challenge beyond bearing — 63

III   Pieces of silver — 141

IV   In tranquillity — 245

Preface

Edmund Gosse began his classic account *Father and Son* (1907) this way: 'This book is the record of a struggle between two temperaments, two consciences and two epochs. It ended, as was inevitable, in disruption.' In a general way much of that applies to the following pages. This is not an autobiography. Rather, it is a memoir (not memoirs) – an account of my father and his consequences.

There are not many memoirs of fathers' relations with sons. Difficulties, after all, are not unusual; they are often transcended (or discarded). Patriarchal structures to some degree entailed them, but also promised inheritance as the heir grew into man's estate.

Implicit in this is a sense of vector. Usually it is the maintenance of property; in Gosse's case, religion – and the way it upheld domestic tyranny. Here, the alignment was with empire and racial dominance.

I had little information about my father's time in Fiji and New Guinea, but soon realised it was incidental to my purpose. *A Führer for a Father*, while a loose title – born of exasperation – nevertheless points to a real linkage. Authoritarianism was the basic assumption on which my father ran his family and faced the world. He was a frontiersman, born in South Africa, with experience of Fiji and New Guinea – and later of Arnhem Land. Everything was firm, definite, unequivocal and hierarchical – in the household, as beyond it.

Re-reading this manuscript, it strikes me that concern about money and wills can, as Australia slides towards greater social inequality, seem like the tiddlywinks of the privileged. But often these function as the hard currency of family relationships, particularly when they are fractured. Beyond that, any family story, if well told, can be of interest and even instructive. This one, among other things, reveals a particularly aberrant instance of patriarchy, expressed in domestic violence towards wives and a persistent antagonism towards a gay son.

Indeed, I was written out of the family story. This book is my attempt to write myself, and my mother, back into it.

A GOOD DEAL OF READING HAS INFORMED THIS TEXT, but I would like to mention some books I have found particularly useful. These are Frank Bongiorno, *The Sex Lives of Australians: A History* (Black Inc, 2012); Ronald Hyam, *Empire and Sexuality: The British Experience* (Manchester University Press, 1991); Bill Schwarz, *The White Man's World (Memories of Empire, I)* (Oxford, 2011); Dane Kennedy, *The Last Blank Spaces: Exploring Africa and Australia* (Harvard, 2013);

Marianna Torgovnick, *Gone Primitive: Savage Intellects, Modern Lives* (University of Chicago Press, 1990); and Howard Morphy, *Aboriginal Art* (Phaidon, 1998). Also useful, for her vivid account of colonial Papua, has been Amirah Inglis, *Not a White Woman Safe: Sexual Anxiety and Politics in Port Moresby 1920–1934* (ANU Press, 1974). Turning to family matters, a valuable second perspective on life at Coppin Street was provided by Peter Coleman, in *Memoirs of a Slow Learner* (Connor Court, 2014). The long quotation on pages 211–12 is from an interview by Geoff Maslen in the *Age*, 17 August 1989. My father's article, 'Mathaman: Warrior, Artist, Songman', appeared in the *Art Bulletin of Victoria* no. 29 (1989) pp. 4–23.

This book was begun while holding a Menzies Fellowship at the Menzies Centre for Australian Studies at King's College, London, in 2014: detachment in England provided the perfect prompt. My thanks to Ian Henderson and Carl Bridge, and to the people at Goodenough College. The third section was written in Hobart, where ideal conditions were provided by my friend Bruce Willoughby. Thanks, too, to Seán Deany.

A number of people have been helpful to me in writing it. In South Africa Bryan Rostron, Tim White and Paul Maylam sought out information. In Tasmania, Carol Bacon provided information on the Spreyton property, while staff at the State Library and Archives were extremely helpful in assisting with other inquiries – which included a perusal of convict records, just in case. Closer to home, Alex Miller, Judith Brett, John Timlin, Sue Murray, Arch Staver (with Bryan Rostron) read and usefully commented on the whole manuscript. Thanks too to Dr Kelvin Adams, for advice on medical matters.

Finally, a word of thanks to all at NewSouth, in particular Phillipa McGuinness, Emma Driver and Jocelyn Hungerford, an adroit and sympathetic editor.

I

A frontiersman marries

How much of us happens before we're born?

Martin Flanagan, *The Age*, 14 January 2012

THERE IS A PHOTO – INACCESSIBLE TO ME NOW – of my father (with Hitler moustache) gravely advancing towards the camera. He has just stepped off Princes Bridge, so part of the city of Melbourne is ranged behind him; he always drew on it more than he cared to admit. In his right hand there's a walking stick, with a silver top: it had been given to his grandfather by a prominent Chinese merchant of the town. Father's firm grip indicates a governing principle of his life, the control of the exotic. Functionally, the stick would turn a limp after a motor accident into a stylised, emphatic strut. It became an instrument of authority.

Some ninety years earlier, in the 1840s, his grandfather had been baptised in what is now styled St James Old Cathedral; this detail was recorded on the fly-leaf of the family Bible. But – apart from the preposterous claim that the man would later be set upon by footpads and murdered in Albert Park – Father rarely spoke of his antecedents. Certainly not of the original Davidson, Henry, who as a bricklayer helped to build the rising city. Rather, there was vague talk of fortunes won and lost on the goldfields (something of an urban myth in mid-twentieth-century Melbourne). Perhaps Henry went to the diggings, perhaps not. Whatever the case, while professing indifference, my father was sufficiently socially aware to cultivate cousins who had gone into the law. A mounted photograph he valued showed their boom-style mansion in Hawthorn, shortly after it was built, with the relatives ranged outside.

The one relative he spoke of admiringly was his Uncle Arch, who seems to have been a freebooter – that is to say, one of the colonial-born who was happy to regard the British Empire as his backyard, advancing his own interests as it expanded. The grandfather ran an import–export business, and may have been undone in the bank crash of 1893. Whatever the case Arch, with Bert (an older brother and my father's father), decided to leave Melbourne for South Africa. Following the recent gold discoveries which led to the mushroom growth of Johannesburg, prospects there were good. Not all Melburnians leaving for goldfields headed for Western Australia; in an unfederated Australia, sailing to the Cape was not much different from sailing to WA – both were British colonies, only South Africa took longer to reach.

Arch would be drawn to the frontier, to the new country being opened up and styled Rhodesia. (It sounded like a province of the Roman Empire, but memorialised the greatest freebooter of them all, Cecil Rhodes.) Arch was photographed on horseback with rifle at the ready and bandolier slapped over his shoulders, patrolling the country in the Matabele War and the subsequent rebellion. Later he went off to the Sudan. But Bert seems to have stayed in South Africa. There is no evidence of what he did there during the Boer War, and little else that has

survived. But from early boyhood I was shown photographs, on thin crinkly paper, dark brown rather than
sepia, of lonely houses on treeless plains, and sturdy iron-
frame bridges flung across rivers sometimes reduced to
sputtering streams. They dried up in winter, I was told.
The bridges had been built by my grandfather, I was
again told. Perhaps he had become an engineer – a term
used at the time with remarkable looseness; at the very
least he would have been an official of the Central South
African Railways, organising materiel and labour. There
were certainly a number of these bridges, all part of the
reconstruction after the Boer War. And the work took him
to some out-of-the-way parts of the country.

One of these was the Marico, a district well known for
its laconic Afrikaners. Bert was working on the construc-
tion of the new railway to Zeerust; a photograph of the
festivities at its opening was a treasured possession. It was
here that he may have met Frieda, his future wife. But it is
also likely that they could have met at Ladybrand, a rising
settlement at the foot of the Maluti mountains. A number
of English-speakers had, since the war, been taking up
farms in the Caledon valley. Bert, having left the railways,
was one of them.

Frieda, who spoke a flawless English, exhibited a
Germanic blend of earnestness and amenability; though
generally good-natured, she did not have much of a sense
of humour. Instead she had a temper: once, when enraged,

she hurled an axe at a Basotho 'boy'. African subservience was simply taken for granted. The Boers had grabbed this territory, adding it to their Orange Free State republic, and had driven the Sotho across the river. They were now no threat. They streamed in to work on farms or the distant mines — but the mountains teemed with them. For all the easy dominance of white over black, colonial life sometimes seemed like riding an elephant.

It was in Ladybrand that my father, James Albert (Jim), was born in March, 1908 — exactly nine months after the Zeerust festivities. He always claimed that 31 March was his birthday — but since for him the truth was always malleable, I strongly suspected 1 April. That would never do, since it would make him a figure of fun. When I finally saw his South African birth certificate, it brought the surprise that actually he was born some days earlier.

Another fudging concerns when the Davidsons left Ladybrand, and indeed South Africa. For Father this was always adjustable. About the age of eleven was a favourite — although he did commit the venial sin of writing after his name in a book, 'Pretoria University 1928'. But it seems the family came to Australia shortly after he was born. Bert's farming and orcharding venture had run headlong into a serious drought; he had not done well. Indeed, around this time, a number of Australians who had gone to South Africa before the war, and were now in poor circumstances, were actively helped to return by the new federal government: Bert Davidson may have been one of them. Certainly the Davidsons left Ladybrand when my father was an infant. Once, as part of a birthday celebration, I gave him an old postcard of the place (sent in the year of his birth). It was a test. He examined the image with an air of affectionate curiosity, but identified nothing.

It seems that Bert – suffering from fever – had gone to Tasmania for a holiday for New Year 1909. He was struck, as were many veterans of imperial climes, by its pleasant summer. The district of Spreyton was tucked in behind the Mersey estuary, which could pass for an antipodean Cumberland; a nearby curling railway line introduced the necessary progressive element. Spreyton was 'going ahead' on the basis of apple-growing. Bert – perhaps with his wife's family money – bought fifty acres of land for an orchard, and was back within three months.

Dignified and affable, and buttressed by Frieda's no-nonsense deliberativeness, Bert soon became a respected leader of a growing community. A newspaper article appeared about the spread of orcharding in the Mersey Valley, taking its bearings from his property. Sensibly, he had avoided planting on the flat land adjacent to the road, since it was marshy; the apple trees were planted on a gentle slope (good for drainage); there were also experimental peaches, plums and quinces. On the crown of the hillock, surrounded by large wattles, stood the homestead. The *Advocate* reporter noted how well tended the property was, and also commented on the seam of coal it contained. That sustained a small two-man mine – also called Illamatha. The name is not an African one; this was to be a new start.

Jim was the only one of the children born in South Africa. Eighteen months later came Hector. Taller than Jim, there was not much likeness: his prominent teeth were often displayed in a friendly smile while he held himself cautiously; a touch of reserve went with his equanimity. At first Hec accepted a natural lieutenancy in relation to his elder brother, who was intellectually quicker. But Jim's behaviour was not predictable: once they climbed a mountain together, and on reaching the summit, Jim swept Hec's cap off his head and threw it down the other side. Puzzled, Hec retrieved it. In time, as Jim moved away, Hec came into his own, as an amateur boxer and a crack shot who did well in shooting competitions. (Later, during the war, he would rise to lieutenant.)

Considerably younger was Laura, the only girl. Partly because she was as strong-willed as he was, Laura attracted Jim's particular derision. He would play tricks on her, a favourite story being how he (and a compliant Hec) had placed a bucket up a tree. 'Pull the rope, Laura', he urged. After some hesitation she did so, and was drenched with water. Having no patience with Laura, Jim had no patience with femininity – his habit of disparagingly imitating women's voices probably began in the wars with his sister. Their scepticism towards each other endured for as long as Laura lived, their relationship oscillating between estrangement and amnesty.

Finally there was Bob, the ill-starred member of the family. Eight years younger than Jim, Bob was not strong; he complained of headaches, had an episode in a mental hospital, and would develop goitre – a very Tasmanian complaint. Surprisingly, he was outgoing, and took part regularly in cycling events, pottering along. A simple fellow, Bert intended the orchard for him.

Jim was not a team player. Money may have been tight, for he was pulled away from school at the age of fourteen. This probably impeded his socialisation. He played in a football team, for a while, but his chosen recreations were more solitary. In addition to mountain climbing, Jim became a marksman, participating in archery, rifle and shotgun contests. But it was boxing he always listed first. Years later he claimed to have been a Tasmanian champion, but that seems to have been Daddish for being able to lick anybody he chose: he was certainly aggressive. Meanwhile his horizons broadened, as he moved away to work on farming properties. For a time he worked in a sawmill, and also on a ketch servicing the islands of Bass Strait. He often made a good impression, and took pains to keep in touch with those he had found to be formative influences.

At the beginning of 1927 Frieda was in a state of advanced pregnancy. When her time came, she went into the Devon Hospital. Complications set in: it proved to be a difficult birth, and shortly afterwards the baby died. Her milk, in Jim's words, 'became infected'; as he told me this over fifty years later, there were tears in his eyes – something I'd never seen before. For his mother died too, missing South Africa to the end. There had not been a silver hair on her head. Bert had an unusually high gravestone erected in the Latrobe cemetery: a monument to her loyalty and gift of expatriation, as much as to the wife and mother of his children. Jim, just nineteen, had a nervous breakdown. Something else – like a romantic disappointment – may have triggered it, but basically it was a response to the loss of his mother. Around this time he was climbing through a fence, and looked back at the house. For a second, in his heightened nervous condition, he saw it standing forlorn and empty – abandoned.

Jim left. For a time he stayed with his hospitable friend Bob Mackenzie on their family farm beyond Burnie, right on the sea; there was a consolatory romance with Bob's sister. Then he decided to go further afield, to Queenstown. The Mt Lyell copper mines were then in full production; set in a lunar landscape, it was an entirely different world from the North-West Coast. There Jim found companionship, roistered, may have drunk a lot and, in reaction, even signed the Pledge – for in later life he was always a moderate drinker. (He probably feared the loss of control.) Queenstown was a small community, packed with incident. It was as well, because the town was isolated. There was no road into the place; only the railway line connected it with Burnie and the world beyond. For something to do, people would go down to the station to welcome the daily train.

Even as he relished life there, Jim was planning the next move. Putting his free time to good purpose, he began attending classes at the School of Mines – in engineering, maths, and machine design. The goal became obvious, even as the Depression began: he would go to Melbourne.

LESS THAN A HUNDRED KILOMETRES FROM SPREYTON LIES one of the loveliest parts of Tasmania. Advancing westwards from Launceston, the old road – sometimes lined with hawthorn hedges – leads you to plains spasmodically dotted with sheep and clumps of cattle; the Western Tiers beyond, often of a uniform blue, are surprisingly trim for a mountain profile. It is the English colonial dream made real. A number of Georgian houses are prominent in the landscape, and two or three villages still have an early-nineteenth-century charm. The one that doesn't, Hadspen, nevertheless retains the shape of its claim to distinction: it is one of the few in Australia that, like a number in England, grew up at the gates to serve a 'great house'.

It is a serene landscape now, but rural Tasmania (at least in the early-settled parts) often gives the impression of still recuperating from its violent first fifty years. My mother's Hay ancestor was partly shaped by them. David Hay arrived in the colony in 1832, as an indentured labourer; an obituary (a bit loose with dates) told of him leading a small party crossing untamed rivers and avoiding 'marauding blacks'. Some time later – but well before the birth of his grand-daughter, Marion – he came to the Westbury district as a tenant farmer on one of the great estates. She would be of the third generation to live there – under the watch of Quamby Bluff – on what had become an independent farm.

Marion had no intention of remaining in the Westbury district. Deep class divisions, all the stronger for there being a considerable Irish Catholic community, spurred her on to develop social ambitions. Marion would claim – over-compensating for convict-clouded Tasmanian origins – that she was a cousin of the Earl of Erroll, who was a Hay; a claim later briskly dismissed by her eldest daughter. Diminutive, unsmiling, and fiery, she crossed the Strait with her sister, and before long appeared with her on the front cover of a Melbourne weekly. The photograph was captioned 'Two Tasmanian Belles'.

Quick-spoken and spirited, Marion had qualities which Norman Tiernan realised he lacked. An early photograph shows him, around the age of thirty, as clear-eyed and good-natured, satisfied with himself and with the world, given his place in it. There were stories on this side of the family, too, of fortunes won and lost on the goldfields, but the Tiernans had also soundly invested in real estate, with astonishing results. Grandma Tiernan – a forceful matriarch – sold a property at the Bourke Street entrance of the Royal Arcade in 1920 for £100 000 (around $7 million today). She then made, on a first-class steamer, the enviable trip Home, something Norman never managed to do.

Norman had done well at school in Latin, and for a time was an accountant. While reliable and dependable, he was also indolent by nature. Being a gentleman – in Edwardian times technically meaning that he didn't have to work for an income – suited him very well. Marion would provide the energy which formerly came from his mother. But there was a problem: she was Presbyterian, he Catholic. She would never agree to her children unilaterally being brought up in the faith. And so a compromise was reached, of a kind not uncommon, then: any boys would follow their father, and any girls would be Presbyterian like their mother. That settled, Marion and Norman were married in 1896, and went off for their honeymoon to the newly fashionable Bayside resort of Sandringham.

In the event, the three children that followed were all girls: Olga, Norma, Tasma. The recurring 'a' of these names, when recited, reveals the musical pulse that ran through the family. This came from the Tiernan side: Norman was

so much a Gilbert and Sullivan fan that he named their
Elsternwick house 'Iolanthe' – only to wince whenever he
heard the postman call it 'I-ole-unth'. (In those days house
names were common, as newer streets often lacked numbers.) Yet it was from Marion that the quickness vital for
a good performer came. In Olga, it combined with her
father's placidity to lead her to the harp, and basically to a
secondary role, producing a softening, sweetening effect. 'I
love harmony', she would say, for by temperament she was
a peacemaker. With Norma, one of the younger twins, that
quickness exploded on the keyboard, producing the bright
melodies of the 1920s, 'Chopsticks' and even honky-tonk.
But the star of the sisters was the other twin, Tasma: her
emotional intensity and spontaneity, allied with an impressive technique, made her an exceptional cellist. She was
the one professional, fortunate in that when she was starting out radio – and radio orchestras – were becoming big.
She toured to Perth a number of times, and developed
quite a following. As one admirer sighed,

> When Tasma plays the 'cello
> My heart joins in the tune:
> So sweet & low & mellow –
> (Now steady there, old fellow!)

And in working-class Footscray, a fan in little Tiernan
Street put up a plaque, naming his house 'Tasma'.

Music was the efficient secret of the household, its real currency, uniting the family as they coped with the dominating and uncompromising mother – to whom it was a matter of indifference. When the gramophone arrived, how they loved it when the man on the cylinders used to announce Edison recordings; and how they would… scamper to the overture to *Zampa*, revelling in the instant gaiety music could afford. Norman's sense of humour, which ran to pulled faces and funny walks, might prolong the mood.

Meanwhile Marion took to croquet – dressing up to the nines in her whites with such enthusiasm that someone derisively called her 'Girlie'. The name stuck. 'Playing ladies', as her daughters styled it, was her preferred milieu. An invitation survives for an 'at home' held on 5 June 1912 – by Mrs Norman Tiernan as President of the People's Liberal Party Women's Section, Elsternwick. We may be sure that her daughters were brought on to provide musical entertainment. Norman took these occasions in his stride; so respectable had he become that his Catholic affiliations gradually faded away. The conscription referenda, the Irish rebellion and the suspicion that the loyalty of his co-religionists could never quite be taken for granted, given their allegiance to the Pope, would do their work. Ultimately, the only flicker of the old attachments was that Norman could never quite turn away a man seeking work when he bore an Irish name.

A virtually bookless household, it was informed by the prejudice of caste. They took their privileged existence for normality: Norman was shocked, when promenading one day with the rest of the family, to be shouted at by a man up a tree, 'Down with the toffs!' *Me? A toff!* Yet he would think it harmless fun to pretend to be doing a line for the maid – just to hear her say, with her speech impediment, "Top it, Midda Tiernan!' A certain lordliness went with the Edwardian style. Once, at the theatre, he was annoyed by a woman talking loudly behind him, and turned round to urge her to be quiet. This time it was she who turned to her companion to say, 'My, isn't he ungovernable!' Imperial assumptions underpinned these attitudes. Late in life Olga, who never went overseas except to New Zealand, would say: 'Australians! They're always striking!'

All three sisters were sent to the Presbyterian Ladies College, of which they generally had fond memories. Its motto from Goethe – 'Without haste, without rest' – would license Olga's thoroughness, and she quoted it often. A liberal institution, it did not insist on overly standardised handwriting, and the three sisters developed their own quite distinctive styles. There was Tasma's, a simple, unevolving Edwardian script, straight up and down; a counterpoint to her impulsive temperament. Then Olga's, both rounded and curt, sensuous with jabs at modernity. And finally Norma's, wavy, with periwinkles of self-involvement.

Olga became the centre of gravity in the family. As Tasma did not get on with Norma – who had the hardness of Girlie without the purpose – she became close to her big sister, and relied upon her. All three – Norma possibly less – adored their father in his benign ineffectuality; and Olga seemed best placed to mediate with the mother. In fact, while doing her best to love her mother, Olga was often alarmed at her behaviour, and quelled by her sharp remarks. As if to clinch a case, Girlie would declare, 'You know what you are!' Easily intimidated, Olga became diffident, socially hesitant; she would not advance unless absolutely sure of her ground. Photos exist of her in large groups of picnickers, at places like Sorrento, Warburton and Cowes; standing with her head to one side, sometimes in a reverie of her own. Yet she had quality, and something of the Hay attack: as well as playing the harp in Melbourne's only (amateur) orchestra, she became a first-class secretary and stenographer, and – more surprisingly – an expert horsewoman. The one broad smile in her surviving photographs was taken when, after a gallop, she was preparing her horse to cross a stream.

Apart from the tugs of romance, it is not surprising that the sisters began to look for a way out. Norma fell for an advertising man, Stan Coleman; since her mother would not approve the match, she arranged to go with him to the registry office and tie the knot there. Tasma was induced to go too, taking along some beau. But somehow Girlie got wind of it: the double absence, and perhaps the strange behaviour of Carrie the maid (who must have known what was afoot) would have alerted her. Once she found out what was going on, Marion swept into the rehearsal room of Alberto Zelman, the kindly conductor: he must do all he could to prevent it. So persuasive was she about the impending double marriage – carrying off his prime cellist as she clumsily parachuted from the Tiernan household – that Mr Zelman accompanied her to the registry office. To Girlie's horror, Norma had already been 'done', and was no longer a Tiernan; Tasma's ceremony was to take place shortly. That was instantly cancelled. Tasma was brought home.

Girlie remained furious about Norma's wedding: it was so much less than the kind of match – or wedding – she wanted for her daughter. Later, with some reluctance, she gave the marriage a limited approval, arranging for a clergyman to come to her home and bless it in a little ceremony. But she was heard to darkly mutter that she hoped there wouldn't be any children.

Olga, as the good daughter, had followed her mother's bidding earlier, with disastrous results. In 1920, when not yet twenty-two, her engagement was announced to a pastoralist on a property near Naracoorte, South Australia. She did not find the man compatible, and the engagement was broken off. Girlie was reluctant to give up on her social engineering; Olga did come to have a gentle romance with a pleasant man who treated her tenderly. But it failed to clinch.

THE TIERNANS HAD BEEN LIVING AT 'LANGI', IN COPPIN Street, East Malvern, for fifteen years or so when Jim Davidson first appeared on the scene, on his motor bike. The house was a little old-fashioned, all red brick and roughcast, with Corinthian clusters of leaves gesturing towards the red-tiled roof. But it had an agreeable corner casement window, and a pleasant veranda, much used in the cool of summer evenings. The grounds were extensive, taking in a couple of additional suburban blocks. There was room for a croquet lawn and summer house, while beyond the dividing lattice and the fernery was a chook run. Here was also kept a buggy, the horse being stabled nearby.

Norman was mellowing, and broadening, into a regular paterfamilias. Another grandson remembers accompanying him to various properties he owned to collect the rent personally; after appropriate pleasantries were exchanged over a cup of tea, he would pull out his fob watch (he had three) and say he must be off. At home, he had taken to sitting in a rocking chair, where he imbibed his opinions from the conservative newspaper *The Argus*. Meanwhile Girlie was bustling about, and never more so than in 1934, when it became known that the visiting Duke of

Gloucester (the King's son), would be going to Ferntree Gully. The Tiernans had a weekender there, and so Girlie was in the thick of fund-raising for a silver tray to be presented to His Royal Highness. Eventually the great day came, and the presentation made. The Duke was a man of few words. 'Thank you!' he said, curtly. The royal family never held quite the same sway over Coppin Street again.

All three daughters were living at home, although Tasma would set sail for Europe a few months after Hitler came to power: she had high hopes of taking lessons from Pablo Casals, and advancing her career overseas. Norma was back home, too, since her marriage with Stan had ended; with her was one of her two little boys, Peter. Tasma was often out, rehearsing or performing, and since Norma was often hitting the high spots, it was Olga – apart from his kindly grandfather – who spent time with Peter. She became so attached to him that years later she would occasionally slip into addressing me by his name. She would then remember with amusement that it was in front of 'Langi' that Peter Coleman, literary figure and conservative politician, had set up a cart and sold copies of his first (home-made) newspaper, *The Lucky Star*.

Olga could appear quite seductive, with her dark eyes and black hair, complete with a winsome curl, contrasting with unusually fair skin and fine, regular features – animated by her quick movements and natural vivacity. At 'Langi', extended on a pile of cushions while her elbow took the weight as she faced the camera, she could look the *femme fatale*. But it was a pose she could not sustain for long: her sense of humour kept breaking through. She thought it funny that a woman would sing – in the standard translation, then, of 'O don fatale', 'Oh, my fatal beauty!'. Beyond that, sex to her ideally was an emanation; the mechanics were absurd and nonsensical. At PLC she had once arranged Wagner's *Liebestod* effectively for a school production, to widespread approval. Unwittingly following Berlioz, she handled coolly the things that are most fiery. She would have died to be told that the piece was a male orgasm rendered as tone poem – or more likely, would have simply said, 'Don't be silly!'

For Jim Olga was a prize worth going for. He could see that she was highly competent, but not altogether confident: a useful combination. And he and Girlie were kindred spirits: they at once responded to the ratbag in each other. (It was about this time that Marion, having a domestic with Norman at Ferntree Gully, suddenly pulled out a red-hot poker from the combustion stove, and held it close to his face.) She didn't care for Olga's suitor Jack, dismissing him as 'a worm' – despite his war wound. By contrast, there was Jim, recently returned from Thursday Island, full of stories. Why don't you get yourself a real man, like Jim Davidson? she asked. But Olga was not to be rushed, and had become quite expert in gently resisting her mother.

Besides, she was enjoying life, and had no great desire to take on such a strong personality, this wild man. So different from Thorold Fink – son of the more famous Theodore – her boss at the *Herald* office: she loved Fink's good manners, his urbanity, his appreciation of her skills as a charming secretary and an accurate typist and stenographer. (They were almost exactly the same age.) And she enjoyed meeting the people who turned up there, years later recalling the novelist Roy Bridges – with whom she got on – and Walter Burley Griffin, in his big, broad-brimmed hat. And Jim Davidson, freshly returned from Thursday Island. So when the Tiernans – perhaps pressed for money – thought of selling their extensive property in Coppin Street to buy four smaller, older ones, Olga decided she would not move the whole way with them. Instead of joining her parents in their new home at 14 Wynnstay Road, Armadale, she would get a small flat nearby.

Suddenly Jim had his motor accident. He was laid up in hospital for nine months, since he had not only broken his leg, but also his pelvis; a kidney had to be removed. Unhesitatingly Olga visited him, frequently. Their relationship steadily deepened. So once he was discharged, the courtship began in earnest. He took her canoeing on the river, and camping in the bush, experiences she had never had before. There is a photo of her in long shorts and a bush hat, standing in front of a tent with her hand placed high on the tent pole. It gives the impression that she was trying out a role, and enjoying it.

But Jim was restless. He had never cared for Melbourne, and having become a qualified surveyor since arriving there, he began looking around for jobs. Jim threw away his stick (metaphorically speaking), lost his limp and was off to Fiji, where he would work as a surveyor on a gold mine. Years later, Olga said to me, when I was setting off on long overseas journeys of my own: 'You Davidsons! You just want somebody to say goodbye to!'

Among Olga's remaining papers is an item in my father's neat printing hand. It's a poem, of only eight short lines. It reads flatly and seems quite perfunctory, until examined closely. 'You are far away', it begins, rising to

Though every hope
May wane and set,
Yet thee I never
Can forget.

It's written from a distance – perhaps a very great distance. Could it be that Jim's second big adventure was that of a man disappointed in love? That he had returned from Fiji, only to find himself still in a stalemate with his beloved? Olga would not commit. His return to the Islands – this time, New Guinea – where he worked for the Standard Oil Company on the headwaters of the Fly River, is perhaps best read this way. Jim had stories about both Island experiences: those of Fiji were more responsive to what he encountered, vivid, romantic. But while he was in New Guinea, he was emotionally distracted.

Jim returned. At Coppin Street he could always count on a warm welcome from Girlie, and so laid siege to her daughter once more. He put the question again to Olga. And pressed her. Desperate, he threatened to take an overdose of morphine tablets if she would not have him. Knowing the kind of man he was, and in a crisis being one more inclined to respond to others' initiatives rather than act decisively herself, the day came when Olga said, 'Yes'. She had learned to live with Girlie; she would learn to live with Jim. Besides, he was undoubtedly fond of her.

On Christmas Eve, 1938, they were married in the Cairns Memorial Church in East Melbourne – a stone's throw from where Olga had been born, and effectively the chapel of PLC. Characteristically, on the marriage certificate Jim ran ahead of himself, giving his age as thirty-one instead of thirty.

FOR A TIME THEY LIVED IN A SEMI-DETACHED FLAT IN A widow's house in a newer part of Hawthorn. Olga continued her job at the *Herald* office, while Jim had taken a job as a draftsman. He was keen to buy a house. One was found in Roseberry Avenue, North Brighton, and bought on terms. Olga was excited about their new home, and although she succumbed to appendicitis and other ailments – forcing her to give up her job – she contributed the floor coverings and furniture.

Olga's enforced domesticity provided the perfect context for her to have a child. It was to this house that I was brought shortly after being born in July, 1942. The birth was not without anxiety: one woman, a stranger, conscious of the Japanese advance in the Pacific, had told a pregnant Olga, 'I wouldn't like to be having a baby, now!' Olga was nearly forty-four – unusually late to give birth, then. Bob Mackenzie's sister Phyll, a trained nurse, came over from Tasmania to help.

About this time a photographer took a joint formal portrait. Jim is almost elegant, standing in a fine coat with hands held by his side, plus his Hitler moustache: with all the rigidity of a toy soldier, he looks at Olga commandingly. He stands at a forty-five-degree angle away from her. She is in hat and gloves, and a heavy overcoat, and sports a fox fur; Olga returns the gaze, warily. Her smile is checked, and not just by the camera. The Zoo, with its exotic contents, would have appealed to Jim as a suitable backdrop. But Olga was beginning to feel captive herself.

Suddenly Jim's attitude seemed to have changed. One day (I'm told), when I was about six months old, he came into my room, stood beside my cot, and said petulantly, 'You get all the attention around here!' Quite suddenly he became stingy. Whereas since the birth he had done the shopping and paid all the housekeeping bills, he now refused to do either, placing Olga on short financial rations. Her own meagre allowance was sucked into running expenses – particularly as he would invite friends round on a weekly basis. Then his sister, Laura, reappeared, a trained nurse now, and was helpful and friendly to her. That soon ended. Jim – resenting a possible female entente aimed against him – quarrelled with his sister, said he didn't want her visiting any more, and forbade Olga to have anything more to do with her.

He was not a happy man. He disliked the draftsman's office, and felt as though his wings had been clipped. This hum-drum domestic life was not for him. His thoughts turned to Fiji where, with the experience of Queenstown under his belt, he had gone in 1935 to work as a surveyor on the Emperor Gold Mine. It immediately became an adventure: he was drawn to the Fijians, enjoyed trekking to remote villages, and began learning their language; their farewell song would hover – he would suddenly sing snatches of it – for the rest of his life. He took on their prejudice against Indians, who instead of being dignified and traditional, he saw as being shopkeepers and agitators. He revelled in the colourful characters he met, including the former Queensland premier EG Theodore and the already published poet RD FitzGerald (also a surveyor), who remained a firm friend.

Then there was New Guinea, more recent. Memories lingered of a Christmas dinner with two others, their camp a platform on stilts, somewhere in the jungles on the headwaters of the Fly River. (He loved remoteness.) A wind-up gramophone, and the strains of 'The man who would woo a fair maid' from Gilbert and Sullivan, which he would croon with light despondency, if he thought of Olga…And of the boy Uau (Wow), a twelve-year-old who attached himself to him, eager to learn, eager to oblige – 'Yes, taubada!' (Master). The perpetual rain; the tins of tropical fruit salad some darned fool had sent from Down South, when there was tropical fruit all around them! And the time when he had *stepped into a clearing, to find a man there, holding himself proudly…*

World War II promised some escape. Jim had already been a member of the armed forces: as a corporal in the Military Engineers (serving as a militia man) and later, when in the Islands, as a member of the Fiji Mounted Rifles. But he may not have enlisted at the outset, and when he did, it was as a Supervisor of Field Survey – a spin on his civilian life as a surveyor. Physically fit, martial in temperament, and with his strong sense of self, he would have found it difficult to follow orders rather than giving them. A confidential report from his superiors, at the end of the war, presents a picture of consistently average performance: Jim was keeping himself firmly under control. (Shortly afterwards a doctor diagnosed him as suffering from hypertension, more deeply than could be attributed to any war service.) He put a bold front on it and was 'wholesomely' self-confident, was noted as being keen to co-operate, but his opportunities for leadership were best kept to 'minor affairs'.

With the Japanese onslaught in New Guinea, Jim was transferred to Victoria Barracks and work in the Engineering Intelligence Section. In the office as in the corridors, he found the company congenial. A number of people there had lived and worked in New Guinea before the war. One in particular, the explorer Mick Leahy, became a friend. They would all swap stories. *One day I came across a native in a clearing in the jungle. He stood there as bold as brass, and looked as though he'd go me. He was unarmed. So I went for him instead, and we fought, hand to hand...* Much later he would claim that he had been parachuted behind Japanese lines in New Britain, but there is nothing in his RAAF record to suggest that. Even so, Jim would have liked Intelligence for its secret men's business. A photo from this time – his favourite – has him jauntily wearing his Flight Lieutenant's cap, smoking a pipe, but looking as though he's enjoying a joke. It was the nearest he ever got to Danny Kaye.

Meanwhile the domestic situation did not improve. Again they were photographed, formally. He stood alongside Olga and the infant of nine months, in uniform; then subsequently cut himself out of the picture. What we are left with (apart from a snippet of his shoulder) is mother and child, the mother tired, anxious, and exuding not so much resignation as an absorbed sadness. The death of Thorold Fink, in a motor accident, dramatised the way things had suddenly taken a turn for the worse.

Jim was always finding fault, and often would come home, frustrated by something or other at the office, and pick a quarrel. He made no attempt to help, but instead constantly went to the pictures. One night Olga went to bed, and the next thing she knew she was being woken by a torch flashed in her face. It was Jim, returning in a foul mood, as he set about bullying her. Doggedly and quietly – and with a self-containment she had developed as a mechanism to cope with Girlie – Olga carried on. (It was almost provocative.) But she became nervy, had shingles, and developed gall stones.

If she thought him occasionally drunk – it probably meant little more than he had had a few too many – it was because Jim had reason to be dissatisfied with the marriage himself. Years later he would say that Olga had lied about her age; he didn't regard that as (so the saying went) a woman's prerogative. And, sure enough, on the marriage certificate her age is given as thirty-five, not forty. That made for a huge reduction in child-bearing prospects, certainly in those days. And he would have gradually become aware that, without consulting him (when she had the child by Caesarian section), Olga's fallopian tubes were tied. That was Girlie's idea, apparently;

her death-wish to the fore. She was always interfering... More seriously, he had wanted lots of children, and now could not have them. News that Hec had died as a Japanese prisoner-of-war on the Burma–Thailand railway had recently come through, while Bob's wife had developed chronic paralysis. It had been left to him to carry on the Davidson name. Now he had been sabotaged.

Meanwhile things on the farm – as the orchard had become – were going from bad to worse. Bob was there alone. Bert had moved to Melbourne – where there was more medical help readily available, and where Laura could keep an eye on him. Then Bob's wife, an invalid, was shifted from the nearby Devon Hospital to distant Hobart for further treatment. Bob's morale had not been improved by his being rejected for military service, as unfit. But he was; he complained of getting tired easily, of breathlessnes, while a goitre looked as though it would require an operation. There was an accident. A gun went off as he was getting through a wire fence and he was killed. He was not yet twenty-nine.

Norman Tiernan was also ailing. He had developed cancer, and had been given a few months to live. As a dutiful daughter Olga was very much concerned to be on hand. But it was at this moment that Jim saw his opportunity – he would go to Tasmania and make a go of the family farm. Away from bosses and suburbia, it at once promised freedom and fulfilment. Olga would go with him, of course. That was the duty of the wife. But like a dog refusing to move, she put out her front legs. There was her father, in his extremity; and given Jim's 'sadistic' behaviour, she was afraid to go with him on to a lonely farm. He kept pressing her. Once when she said she didn't want to go, he grabbed her violently — in front of three-year-old me. I apparently rose to the occasion — then or a little later — telling him, 'You shouldn't hit a *girl!*' For he continued to terrorise her. On the way to Olga's father's funeral, he drove at top speed, recklessly, refusing to let her get out. And once, when they were at home, he started laughing manically, declaring he had gone mad. 'You'd better ring the police', he kept saying. Olga was glad when — since they could use the money — the daughter of some old Tasmanian friends came to board with them. That quietened things down a bit. For the sake of harmony, and her little boy, she was prepared to put up with the single women he brought to the house, expecting her to entertain them.

MEANWHILE JIM'S WORK, NOW WITH THE FORESTS Commission, involved road-building near Marysville as well as map-making in Melbourne; he experienced rare job satisfaction. Jim seemed to be aware that he should be more stable, and even agreed to go and see Olga's old school-friend Lil Jorgensen, a psychologist. He used his persuasive powers to great effect. Lil, he would say later, had said there was nothing wrong with him; instead, she thought she should have been examining Olga. A verdict not so surprising, given that she had submitted herself to the authority of Justus of Montsalvat – a man who painted more self-portraits than Rembrandt, with rather less distinguished results.

Olga had two uncles who lived together in a house at Mt Eliza, tucked in a gully overlooking the sea. Nearby stood the old homestead of 'Earimil', its flaking white paint offset by a massive stand of black-green cypress pines; up the hill, as far as the eye could see, spread red canna lilies. Its atmosphere was strong, haunting; my first real experience of place. Jim must have been gripped by it too, because he bought a block of land nearby, and – as a preliminary to building a house – put up a garage. The Tiernan brothers became a forward base.

One day Olga went for a walk, down the picturesque track that crossed the creek, and came across a house – a Californian-style weatherboard, again surrounded by massive cypresses, and prefaced by a grand staircase. A woman was moving about the large garden: they began chatting. The house was about to be put on the market. It set Olga thinking. Perhaps 'Moonya' might solve a problem, through compromise: Jim clearly wanted to live in the country, yet from here he could still manage to go on a daily basis to his job in Melbourne. Receptive to the idea, Jim went over to see the house, made an offer,

and got a bargain. We moved in briskly, at the beginning of 1949; and indeed *on* the mother and daughter,
who stayed there uncomfortably until they could find a
new place. The need for the six-year-old to start the new
school year at Frankston State would have been a strong
argument.

Jim seems to have made some effort to turn over a new
leaf. Olga was given two large musical parties: many old
friends (most of whom I had never seen) came down from
Melbourne. Tasma played the cello; there was piano music
(of a restrained kind), and a violinist or two. Olga played
the harp: rare public performances. She was happy. In her
own mind she was re-enacting the great musical parties
of Louise Dyer (for whom Tasma had regularly played) a
generation earlier.

At some point Olga and Jim's relationship ceased to be
sexual. It was all over within a few months of coming to
'Moonya', as one day the spare room next to mine became
Mummy's bedroom. Mine was originally a sunroom, with
a wonderful view across the paddock I regularly diagonal-
ised every morning – including cold winter ones, amidst
the chortling of magpies – as I walked to catch the bus
that took me to school. But it could only be entered via
Olga's bedroom; and so, while my things remained in the
sunroom, I was directed to sleep in the other twin bed,
with my father. The frontiersman was recreating the tribal
men's hut.

It went further than that. In addition to the usual encouragements, he gave me things which he should not have done: at the age of seven or eight I was incapable of looking after them properly. These included a sword stick, that is to say a walking stick that contained the sword within it. Playing around, I got dirt in it, and it wouldn't close properly: end of disguised weapon. Similarly, he gave me not one or two Fijian stamps, but all of them, including many duplicates – then got annoyed when I swapped them. A magnificent one-pound English stamp, a rarity, he also gave me, and of course it got torn. Believing that I might become another version of himself, he was a doting parent. He wanted me to place him well above a small boy's natural feeling for his mother, indeed make me the junior partner in an alliance against her.

Jim's aggression simmered most of the time. It yielded the occasional comic turn when he took to a chook with an axe, and the headless bird ran frantically around the yard. But – in an equivalent of troop manouevres – he might go there and crack the stockwhip – sometimes connecting with the dog, who might have annoyed him. As he bounded away in pain, Spot's fearfulness was a disturbing sight.

Meanwhile Jim reverted to his tyrannical treatment of Olga: starving her for money – easier in a time of rising inflation. She had to borrow from her sister to buy new clothes. At the same time he refused to allow her to rent out a section of the house to provide income. He didn't want strangers in the house, he said. For a time he allowed Girlie's aged domestic servant to come, since she could no longer be kept on at Wynnstay Road and had nowhere else to go. Amanda lasted only a few months. But Olga had at least broken the ban on having other adults living there. The house was isolated, and she felt the need for another adult presence when Jim was away. Since he was planning a trip to outback New South Wales in the Buick – nailing Spot's box to the running board – he gave the idea a curt nod. None of the tenants were to last very long.

Jim soon saw that 'Moonya' gave him an opportunity to phase his withdrawal from the marriage. By the end of our first year there he had given up the long daily trek to Melbourne. Roseberry Avenue had a bungalow out the back; that became his headquarters during the week, 'Moonya' the weekender he had originally thought of building at Mt Eliza. He could carry on with whom he chose, unknown to almost everyone. That began.

One wintry night in 1950 the phone rang. There had been an accident. Jim was in a car with a Forests Commission colleague, on the Princes Highway near Warragul. Visibility was poor; they crashed into a petrol truck. For his small boy the details were piled on – the truck went up in flames, the other man was driving (of course), and there he was, with a broken leg for the *third* time. It was certainly serious; as in 1934, he had concussion. On the domestic front, once he returned home from hospital, things went from bad to worse.

Previously Olga had tended to regard Jim's attacks as interruptions to normal transmission; he lacked 'self-control', she'd say. Once, when we were seated having a meal with Tasma, Jim, irritated by something Olga had said, struck her on the face. There was a stunned silence: everyone behaved as though nothing had happened. But the threatening behaviour became harder to ignore. He began throwing food and crockery on the floor – he had done that before – but now, when crossed, would hammer the wall with both fists.

At the beginning of 1950 we had gone to Mornington to see a film, set in an English public school. The initiations and the bullying shown there – with older boys picking on younger ones – terrified me, and I asked them to promise I would never be sent to such a school. No dear, my mother assured me. But a carbon copy of such a place was where I would be heading. Olga had become concerned to get me away from the unhealthy atmosphere and Jim's 'bad example', so told him that I was 'becoming difficult to handle owing to the unhappiness in the home'. I suspect she also had a mother's instinct for these things, and when she described me as 'highly strung', that might have included being gay.

Olga was readily sold on Mentone Grammar School. The Principal, Jeffrey Thorold, who merely owned it (he employed a headmaster) was well spoken, and parted his hair in the centre as eligible men did in her youth. Besides, his surname echoed the first name of her beloved boss: she was influenced by such things. Jim saw fidgety hands and a superior English manner trailing into effeminacy. But he was beginning to see that having me out of the way could have its uses.

By now he was telling Olga that she should clear out. All those who had lived with the couple over the years had warned her to take care. The outgoing owner of 'Moonya' was particularly blunt: 'If ever you are found strangled', she said, 'we'll know who to hang!' People wondered why she continued to put up with it. But her pride was involved: she could recall Girlie saying to her husband, when Norma parted from Stan Coleman, 'Divorce is an ugly word, Norman!' She had made a bad marriage, and until the 1960s divorce still carried stigma. Shame would be added to failure. Besides, what would happen to her son? She was anxious to provide a proper home, and kept hoping against hope that the turbulence might disappear...one fine day. But Jim was not Girlie; the disruptive forces were more primal.

One night, as I lay in bed, I could hear them having a row in the kitchen. There were a number of shouts, perhaps a yelp; enough to make me get up to see what was going on. Gingerly I entered the kitchen: empty. Then I heard a sound from the adjacent tenants' kitchen, close to the back entrance. It was Jim, breathing heavily as he lay on the floor. 'Dad!' I cried. I looked around. 'Where's Mum?' In a gasping, exhausted voice, he said, 'She's gone!', and pointed to the open door.

Next morning I was sent over to some friends' place, where she was staying. Years later I learned that he had suddenly declared he wanted to sell 'Moonya', and build elsewhere in Mt Eliza. They would start again from scratch: making a profit (as well as a clean break) was part of the plan. Olga resisted, saying that she didn't think it was a good idea after his accident. He grabbed her roughly and knocked her to the floor. She ran out, into the darkness and the rain, stumbling across unmade streets as she went, afraid that he might follow. But instead he decided to put on a gala performance for me.

Jim was counting on mother love to overcome marital grievance. I remember the statuesque woman Olga was staying with, and could tell it was a serious matter because she was so solemn. Olga listened, unusually gentle (I would now say subdued). I pleaded with her to come home; not quite nine, I yearned for 'harmony' even more than she did. The friend surprised me by being reluctant to let her go. But Olga allowed me to walk her back. While I did not believe that she had attacked him – as I was meant to – I had no idea that the opposite was the case. Nor ever did, until I read documents after she had died.

JIM DID GIVE OLGA A SORT OF APOLOGY WHEN SHE returned, but no sooner had it been uttered than he said, 'Oh, but it's too late, now'. Things were simply restored to what they were before; the downward trajectory continued. Some old Queensland friends came to stay, indeed to board; but they so disapproved of Jim's behaviour that they swung their affections to Olga, told him so, and left. Other visitors fell away: Jim's behaviour towards her made them feel compromised.

He did not let up with bullying and terrorising her. There was more zany driving, constant rough handling, and on one occasion he almost realised the prophecy of Moonya's outgoing owner. Entering Olga's room, he pushed her onto the bed, grabbed her by the throat and said, 'Now we are alone, I will finish you…I'd gladly swing for you!' She felt he was merely trying to frighten her, enjoying being sadistic. But it wasn't just brinkmanship. He had asked for a divorce, saying that he had found 'a good, tough woman who was willing to work hard, and do what she was told'.

Not surprisingly, Olga sickened under the onslaught. In the words of one of the tenants, Jim was 'crucifying' her. A nerve rash appeared on her face, and she was developing a thyroid complaint. On one occasion even Jim noticed a pulse beating in her throat. She decided she had to go on a holiday – getting a medical certificate to vouch for the authenticity of the need – and went and stayed with a friend.

Once away, she could not bring herself to go back permanently – and legal advice to that effect had been added to the doctor's. Olga decided to stay in town, at her mother's, and quickly filled a position as a stenographer. She had been careful to keep up her shorthand. One evening Jim appeared at the door of Wynnstay Road, again using me as a bait: I was to have my ninth birthday, and he had arranged a kiddy party in Frankston. She should come. Almost immediately he announced that he was selling 'Moonya', and wanted her help in preparing it for sale. She agreed to come down, at weekends.

So there was a convergence, then: he turned up from the Roseberry Avenue bungalow, myself from school for the Saturday, and Olga from the dubious refuge of Girlie's, to do the laundry, cook, and help prepare the house for sale. She did this partly to keep up appearances – it was what one did. Beyond that, she had a simple faith. Her place was with her 'little boy' (as she infuriatingly kept referring to me till I was twelve) – and he should feel the same. Then we would be a 'normal' family. In this there was a streak of stubbornness. She had no idea of the forces and impulses driving Jim – which only increased his sense of frustration.

Meanwhile Jim pressured her to sign a contract of sale for 'Moonya', in which she would receive one-quarter of the proceeds. She agreed. He soon said he needed her quarter-share so that he could buy a suitable house. She hesitated, but once there was a phone call from his solicitor asking her to sign the documents (such a nice man…), she complied. Olga still believed 'my husband would do the right thing'. But he had no such intention. Worse, to allay any apprehension he said that – since he was working, and she now was not, owing to increasing illness – she might act as scout for a possible home. She agreed, but it was he who found a house in Monash Avenue, Balwyn.

The time came to leave 'Moonya'. Claiming nerves, Jim said he needed a couple of weeks to himself. My school break-up occurred at this time; both parents came, and I was looking forward to the new home. But we drove to Wynnstay Road first. 'Mummy has to look after Grandma', said my father, 'and will not be coming with us'. 'I'm sick of this', I said. 'I want Mummy to be with us, too.' But she was dropped off, and we drove to Monash Avenue. It was almost a fortnight – Christmas Day – before I saw my mother again.

Meanwhile Olga had discovered that her thyroid gland was in a toxic condition. An operation would be necessary, the sooner the better. Anxious to see me before she went into hospital – and to make sure my clothes were in order for a holiday – she turned up at Monash Avenue early on New Year's Eve. Jim was not pleased to see her. He bullied her, and ranted; she began trembling all over. When I was called away to eat some stew, she returned to my bedroom, and continued darning socks.

Then he ordered me to bed: she went into the kitchen. I hardly spoke with her. Feeling poorly, Olga went to make herself a cup of tea before setting off to catch the tram home. But Jim switched off the jug and ordered her out of the house.

Jim did make a few paltry gestures later, as she went into hospital. Because she was run-down, and despairing, Olga feared she might not come through the operation, and said so. She delivered her own last rites in a letter intended for me, full of sweet resignation and concern. Not once did he take me to see her.

Instead, I was removed from the scene. I found myself in the custody of a sour middle-aged couple who ran a superior guest house at Mount Macedon. If I said anything to Arthur, a silent man, he usually managed to counter it with a disapproving remark; his wife Mavis could have been the sister of Dickens' Miss Murdstone. She was the manageress, to whom 'British-born persons' (that is, Anglo-Celtic Australians) would 'apply' to stay. In a small back kitchen I was forced to eat food (even desserts) I did not like. Elsewhere, if I were caught reading, the book would be snatched away. I was not allowed out. I was not allowed to talk to the guests. At 'Derreweit' there was nothing to do but wander aimlessly in the large garden. Later I heard that it had been laid out by Baron von Mueller, but its now tangled beauties were lost on me. I had no idea of what was going on. With the innocence of childhood –

and inured by boarding school – I basically accepted the situation, greeting my father exuberantly when he visited me at weekends. I pleaded for some relaxation of the rules and, a fortnight or so after being sent there, was allowed to walk as far as the shops. By then Jim figured the new Olga-less order would be safely in place: she had left town to convalesce with some friends on a farm.

There was a third victim of these goings-on. Once Dad told me that Spot had disappeared, and that he had found him near Genazzano Convent, a couple of miles away. What he did not know was that the dog had followed Olga in the tram as far as he could. She had fed him, been kind to him; he missed her. Once more he ran away, looking for her. I would never see him again.

BACK FROM THE COUNTRY, OLGA TOOK UP PERMANENT residence at Wynnstay Road. Girlie would soon go into a home. There would be no more conversations like the only one I ever had with her, when I was seated at the end of her bed and she enjoined me to admire the beautiful lady over there (indicating the wardrobe mirror), while talking of her romance with the Prince of Wales. (Very disconcerting for an eight-year-old.) But Tasma was there, drifting about disconsolately when not practising on her cello. Although depressed since the death of Norman and her contracting tuberculosis, she could provide sympathetic company. Olga was still not fit to work, and relied on a meagre weekly allowance from Jim.

Hers was now a flatter reality: at the beginning of 1952 she had touched bottom, but knew she would survive. Part of her low spirits must have arisen from the sheer exhaustion that would have set in once she realised the constant tension was now over. And once I was back at boarding school, she could count on seeing me once a fortnight, since Jim agreed they would have me on alternate weekends. She began to drift towards religion, which would shape her belief in goodness and give some firmness to her life.

Now she had to recognise what had happened to her, deconstruct some of her assumptions. Not easy; a statement written for her lawyer, narrating the whole sad story, reveals a recurrent disappointment that Jim would not treat her well – 'He came to see me only 2 or three times during the 2½ weeks I was in hospital', she recalled, bringing 'only a bottle of lemonade nothing else'. A poor return for the daily visits she had made to his bedside at the time of 'the accident'. She was a dutiful wife; why couldn't he be a dutiful husband?

At that juncture, nothing could have been less likely. He had two women on the go, and seems to have alternated them. One was the daughter of the Mount Macedon jailers; a toothy piece who displayed her bust like a built-in trophy, and didn't have a great deal to say. Once she came with my father to see me off on a bus journey. She then gave me a watch, with lots of smiles but so few words that it seemed a declaratory act – and a bribe. Perhaps my lifelong aversion to wearing a wrist watch began that day. The other, Claire, I never saw, at least not till the day of my father's funeral. She then struck me as pleasant and gently resilient – a 'good sort'. And she told me, as generous to him as to me, how he had ended their affair by saying that his first duty was to his son. She said this a few times, with such sincerity that for a time I believed it – as a new and mitigating aspect of him I had not seen. But eventually I realised that once again he had used me – as a cover for returning to the buxom one.

But Claire was my mother's bogeywoman, and, after having consulted a lawyer – and drawn up a statement backed by supporting correspondence – she hired a private detective. Olga went with him and his wife to Monash Avenue, to point out the house. The detective subsequently returned a number of times, to ascertain the pattern of comings and goings, once overhearing a conversation (a long one) on 'male perverts'. Eventually, while his wife watched the bedroom from a parked car, he advanced on the house with an assistant. His report is worth quoting, as it captures the chill surrounding sexual morality in the depths of the Cold War:

I rang the front door bell and a man's voice, coming
from the vicinity of the bed-room said, 'Who's there?' I
said, 'I wish to speak to Mr Davidson'. A light came on
in the bed-room and a man opened the front door after
a short delay…He was wearing pyjamas covered by a
check woollen dressing-gown. I said to him, 'This is a
divorce raid', and I passed him and entered the house
followed by my wife and Mr Jones. I entered the front
bed-room and saw a woman – whom I had seen draw
the blinds of the bed-room earlier – lying in the bed
on the side furthest from the door. She sat up in bed…
and [I] said to her, 'You are Miss Claire Lines. You have
been committing repeated adultery with James Albert
Davidson, a married man. What have you to say?' The
woman appeared dazed and made no reply. I repeated
what I had said to her, but she did not reply. The side of
the bed next to the woman had the clothes thrown back
and I felt that side and found it was warm as a person's
body would have left it. There were men's trousers and a
shirt on a chair beside the bed and a man's shoes on the
floor on the side of the bed nearest the door. I turned to
Mr Davidson and said, 'You are James Albert Davidson'.
He said, 'Yes.' I said, 'The woman in bed here is Miss
Claire Lines and you have been committing repeated
adultery with her.' He said, 'Yes.' I said, 'We are here
on behalf of your wife. I am a Private Investigator. This
is my wife and this is my assistant…Your wife intends

proceeding against you for cause of adultery with this woman. Is there anything else which you wish to know?' He replied, 'No'. I then said to him, 'Goodnight'. He said, 'Goodnight', and then we left.

In the event, Olga shelved the idea of divorcing him. She knew how ruthless and shrewd Jim could be, and wasn't sure he would not find a way to gain custody of her son. Better the continued stalemate and division of my time between them. She also became worried that, should she divorce him, then Jim would remarry, have children, and that this could imperil my prospects of inheritance. As the years passed, the religious sanction against divorce came to count for more, too. While they did not prohibit it as Catholics did, Anglican priests nonetheless refused to perform a second marriage if a previous partner were still alive. Remaining Mrs Davidson acknowledged her history – explained the child – and alluded to a deeper identity. To cut the link, now that she was in her mid-fifties, would be less of a renewal than a renunciation.

At this point Olga was seeing a lot of Norma, who had recently remarried. She could do with her brightness, and could accept the sudden withdrawals. Under the amiable eye of Perce, who seemed to be forever sitting in armchairs or on verandas, taking it easy, Norma ran a boarding house in St Kilda and later a guest house in Warburton. Her personality blossomed: she found form as a good manager, could entertain guests in the lounge by her zestful piano-playing, and enjoyed the semi-public exist- ence – while having enough of Olga's subversive sense of humour to relish its absurdities. 'What'll you have, dear', she asked me when I arrived there the first time: 'Ham, ram, lamb, beef or mutton?' No better send-up of the heavy guest-house cuisine of those days could have been devised. So Christmas 1953 was a jolly one. In the guest- house photograph taken shortly afterwards (an institution of the time, with the proprietress cast as headmistress) Olga can be seen – standing towards the back, it is true, but content and lightly beaming. She has her mojo back.

MEANWHILE I HAD SETTLED IN AT MENTONE GRAMMAR. As an eight-year-old, the first term was the hardest, getting used to sleeping in a dormitory: with the blankets rolled back in the morning, the beds looked like rows of opened sardine tins – once the sprats emerged. I was friendless, it was sterile. Only one other boy from my class was there, and he moved about in a daze.

In second term I was moved from Junior House to B Dorm. It was in the main part of the school, and a pro- motion. Most of the boys there were a little older; I was in some dread. There was only chicken wire and wallop- ing shutters to keep out the cold. The beds were ranged in bunks, the boarding school equivalent of tenements.

They were separated by a shelf with a few hooks underneath, covered by a striped cloth. In no sense was it a home; the dormitories were out of bounds during the day. Years later I would see another dorm rather like it – on Robben Island.

Jim's long arm reached even here. When, at the beginning of 1954, I was a polio suspect, he came to visit me in the school dispensary. He was horrified to find that it had no flywire door. So he rang Mr Thorold, and threatened to call in a health inspector: an appropriate door was put in within twenty-four hours. Later, ever setting the pace, he demanded (without reference to me) that I should be allowed to stay up longer, and do prep with seniors. The school acceded. I was twelve and didn't know quite what to do, since we were placed in a room with a teacher (himself sore at being kept in) who would maintain strict silence. Staying up meant I was entitled to a supper of tea and bread and jam – always an object of envy for younger boys. Understandably, this special treatment earned the resentment of my dorm-mates. I would quietly go to my bed at the later hour, and find it short-sheeted, or subject to other minor sabotage. Quietly the experiment was abandoned.

At the same time, Jim's meanness could expose me to ridicule. Since he believed that boys should not wear long pants until they turned fourteen, he was obdurate in resisting the demands of his relatively tall son. (Presumably short pants – virtually gone now – were cheaper.) Subject to considerable jeering, I was almost the last boy in the class to make the change. Around the same time, he paid a tailor to convert an old overcoat of his. It was heavy, old-fashioned, inappropriate, and quickly dubbed by me 'The Pocket-sized Continent'. After I had worn it once or twice in his company, he got the point and agreed I should have a new one. Another cost-saving device was his insistence that I should sharpen razor blades by rubbing them up and down the inside of a glass. Oh, and I should always use cold water – so as not to bring the blood to the surface. I was being asked to replicate the conditions he had shaved under, because of scarcity, on the headwaters of the Fly.

When I was about fifteen, and spending a weekend at school, I zoomed around the grounds on a bike, and at an adjacent tennis court saw the terror of us all, the Assistant Headmaster, smiling and chatting as he went on to play a match. He even had a greeting for me. It was at that moment I realised that I had a problem with my father. He was never relaxed and comfortable – not even as John Howard understood the term. Even earlier, I had a shock on first seeing a Holbein portrait of Henry VIII. It was…Dad…magnified. For my father had something of that presence, and a powerful chest, above which there was a similar square face, and – although I could not have named it then – a coldness in the eyes.

The punitive was never far away. 'You've got a lot to say!' he'd declare, when I would answer the latest charge. I had no standing before the court. Then the assault would begin: things ripped out of context, twisted, piled on each other – to show what a thorough-going worthless fellow I was. One day I must have said something about harshness: he replied that he was treating me as other people would, in preparation for the real world. Home was no refuge.

I can't say I was belted all that much – probably less than a dozen times in the Monash Avenue years. But these occasions were totally unpredictable. Once he met the bus bringing me from Mentone, looked straight to my shoes – which were dirty – and said he would belt me when we got home. I tried to explain: there hadn't been time to clean them. Mr Thorold had gone on and on with announcements at the end of boarders' breakfast, and I feared I would miss the bus, keeping him waiting for three-quarters of an hour until the next. I would have to make a dash for it...But Dad was not interested. So our day together began with the belting.

Even an outing might turn sour. When I was eight we went to Benalla, and stayed the night in a pub. It was an exciting, new experience. As we were walking along the main street, I stopped, and pulled out my handkerchief to blow my nose. Out came a two-shilling piece, which hit the ground on its side and rolled towards a grate. It disappeared. I was heartbroken – it was a week's pocket money. Since I would soon be back at school for the week, I asked Dad if he could give me some more money. No, said he, you should have been more careful.

The assumption was always identity of purpose. At the age of eleven, I was taken to see a vocational guidance officer. He spoke to each of us separately. There was a Japanese print on the wall, of an arch; apparently we both commented on it on entering the room. The man was surprised; Dad took it as confirmation. Then we saw a film once, which involved a boy hanging on for dear life to a wire strung across a ravine. His father yelled out encouragement: Hold on...! How would you react in this situation? Dad asked. Don't know, I replied, truthfully. It was too far beyond my experience — and perhaps I wouldn't have entirely trusted that voice. It was not the answer he wanted. I had failed to endorse the regime.

That was what was expected. I was told, repeatedly, never to correct him in public. And I always had to watch my p's and q's. Otherwise, when I'd almost forgotten an incident where I hadn't, back it would come some days later, now the centrepiece of a log of claims to show how unsatisfactory I was. Once, with the verbal exuberance of a thirteen-year-old, I said something that annoyed him as we were walking by the seashore. He stopped us in our tracks, and analysed what I had said with a totally inappropriate seriousness — so markedly that I remember thinking that there can only be a few more years of this, thank goodness. Much, much later, I read the historian AP Thornton, who remarked that everybody has experienced imperialism – it's called childhood; I rose from the desk and danced around the room. For the authority was so oppressive that sometimes the line crossed had been invisible. On one occasion my father taxed me with having told his woman that Bob his brother had suicided. Suicided? It was news to me. I had mentioned the accident, going through a fence; Margaret had put two and two together. But childhood innocence 'cut no ice' with Jim. There was no excuse for 'shooting your mouth off'.

And, like Kim Jong-un, there were dynastic pretensions. Once, when he lay down beside me on the bed – as he would occasionally until I was about seven – he spoke of my name, and how I was the sixth Jim Davidson in a row (not even remotely true). There were also secret signs. How I was to ring from the bus stop when being picked up – five rings, and then stop. (It saved money.) And one day he produced two little stones. These are from the top of Table Mountain (Cape Town), he said. You have one, and I have one. If ever you are in real danger, send it to me. I'll do the same. I never saw his again; I lost mine.

BUT IN SOME WAYS HE WAS A GOOD PARENT. ONE DAY AT 'Moonya', gypsies came up in the dinner conversation. I persisted with questions, until he took me to the little toolshed behind the fuschia. It was small and dark in there; he went in, and emerged with a large book. It contained a section, 'The History of the Gypsies'. Thus I received the first volume of a set – *Richards Topical Encyclopedia*. The other fourteen were withheld – in the toolshed chest – and 'bought' on a regular basis from the pocket money I made from mowing the lawn. It was a sensible way of ensuring that each volume was, if not treasured, carefully examined. None were to exceed the pleasures of the first, with its stories of Mesopotamia and the ancient world, tellingly illustrated by dramatic nineteenth-century history paintings. Perfect for an inquiring child. Steadily I acquired them over a couple of years, always passing over the science and technology ones. In a moment of exasperation, he gave me those remaining volumes in a desperate spurt of encouragement. They would remain (almost) virginal.

He also had a capacity to surprise, and sometimes to delight. One Friday evening, when I made my way from school to his office in the Forests Commission, he announced that he had something to show me. We got in the car and drove a short way, down an unprepossessing street. There was a shoe factory, but also a small patch of bush. We went over. Behind it was a very old house. Locked up; we couldn't go inside. This, he said, is the original Government House. I scarcely believed him; but it was Jolimont, then in its original location. Another time he produced a rare dish – a bird, oily, salty, and amazingly tasty. It was mutton bird, which he would have eaten many times in his Bass Strait days.

His interests were broad, especially in the visual arts, where they were as yet unfocused. He took me to a contemporary Italian art exhibition (rather blobby), the Herald Art Show (blobby in a different way) and the Hiroshima Panels (despite a Communist taint). Above the kitchen table was placed a picture of Picasso, his arms held close to a table, with croissants placed where his hands might have been expected to be. Jim spoke of Cyril Connolly's *Horizon* with admiration. So with some justice he thought of himself as being a bit of a bohemian. This extended to befriending a middle-aged English couple who were music teachers – the art to which he normally had a take-it-or-leave-it attitude. His record collection was as eccentric as his books – everything from a Chinese song from Cairo to Mozart sung primly by a vocal quartet.

There was also, of course, a geographical spread about him, an intense curiosity about other places. I had that too, encouraged by the map of the world he placed on his six-year-old's bedroom wall. (As things turned out, for a long time my sense of Melbourne was weak, while that of the rest of the world was abnormally strong.) Gradually, immersed in the tides and eddies of fluctuating truths, I came to be less lateral by inclination, and increasingly oriented to the vertical: history represented depth, and ascertainable truths. But because the call of the exotic was so strong in him, the one way he was truly generous was in enabling me to travel.

At the end of 1954, when I was twelve, he took me to Papua–New Guinea. It exerted a strong pull on him, still. He subscribed to the *Pacific Islands Monthly*, and was excited by Colin Simpson's *Adam in Plumes*; he got wind of the coffee boom then under way in the Highlands, and decided to see for himself. The journey was supposed to take a day and a half, but took more than twice that – air travel in New Guinea was a bit of a gamble in those days. We travelled to the centre of the new industry, and pushed beyond to stay in the Wahgi Valley. I travelled with him to plantations, and wrote a summary for him as to the comparative advantages of producing high-class arabica coffee compared with cocoa. And, when he went off on a further expedition, leaving me to stay in the Goroka Hotel, I noted two things that would be of lasting interest. I had heard settler talk of minister Hasluck ('Arselick') appeasing the United Nations, and repeatedly of their fear that the Indonesians would take over Dutch New Guinea – *first*. The anger arose from their paradise being threatened. There they now were, lined up outside the District Commissioner's Office, waiting for the detailed announcement of blocks of land that were up for lease. It was one of the last land-grabs of British – or sub-British – imperialism. And I also got a glimpse of the mentality which helped sustain it. One day I walked into a shop, and the Australian woman behind the counter began talking to me in pidgin. Once I realised it would flow on, I said I couldn't understand what she was saying. She stopped suddenly and apologised. But it was plain that to her a white boy and a native 'boy' – a fully grown man – were virtually interchangeable.

It was a measure of Jim's dissatisfaction with life that – in addition to his job at the Forests Commission – he was always engaged in some business venture, preferably combined with the idea of leaving Melbourne. Apart from feeling confined here, the winters brought bronchitis. So he did invest in New Guinea for a time, though did not go to live there; and toyed with moving to Merimbula, running a caravan park, or a series of cabins at Coles Bay in Tasmania. Then there was the little airline he owned, freighting goods to the Bass Strait islands, and his interest in one of the last boarding houses in Melbourne's city block. He was always on the look-out for ways to make money. One day he announced that he was going to collect stamps. Oh goody, I said as an excited eleven-year-old, glad that he had seen the light! I was soon brought up sharply. 'I'll be collecting in an adult way', he announced. But he soon gave it away: perhaps he found you couldn't.

Because he was so entrepreneurial – and because he had the frontiersman's generous ration of paranoia – there was always a threat. The first time I heard the word 'pregnant' was when he was describing a blowfly buzzing around the dinner table: immediately there'd be a swarm. And at the age of seven I had some trouble distinguishing starlings (nesting in the spouting) from Stalin − both were menacing. Around that time, perhaps a little earlier, we were crossing the road in front of a stationary tram. Dad points out the tram driver: 'He's a Communist!' Little boy looks up, and sees a man blank-faced and indifferent, terrible in his elevation and implicit power. Later, there was a picture in the paper of literary figures Clem and Nina Christesen, arriving for their interrogation by the Petrov Commission. I saw a rather old, stooped man; but, said my father, they're Communists. Reds at the university. Not surprisingly, then, although his love of the exotic took him into the Immigration Reform Group, alarm at its innate radicalism soon led him to drift out of it.

ONE NIGHT IN OCTOBER 1957, THE BOARDERS WERE ALLOWED to go outside to glimpse Sputnik, the first man-made object to be launched into orbit around the earth. It was a tiny pinprick, moving with measured persistence across the sky. Younger boys expressed disappointment; the satellite was so tiny, there was nothing sensational about it at all. But it was a portent.

The Soviets, and science. Suddenly these two things were foregrounded. A week or two later we had to choose which stream we would take for Leaving Certificate (Fifth Form). One boy, later a distinguished clergyman, turned his back on his natural bent and chose science, until talked out of it by the Assistant Headmaster, who also taught history. His teachers couldn't take the strain, he joked.

But science it was going to be, for me. The school authorities made no attempt to talk Jim out of this decision; they knew what he was like. Instead – in an act of inspired schoolmastering – they decided to comply, more or less. I remember a conversation with the short-tempered history master, he whose name, Ivey, I had turned into Ivan the Terrible. He was surprisingly realistic and friendly: I might do *one* history subject without attending his classes. Meanwhile, I applied myself to maths and physics and chemistry, honestly. The first-term results were a rout. Eagerly I set upon the mark the maths teacher had given me for my paper (an emphatic failure), and took it up to him to correct it. 'Well, it wouldn't make any difference, would it?' How right he was. But it was a pity I couldn't fail *him*, for arithmetic.

The world had become rather flat and grey. I took a job near my mother's, as a petrol pump attendant on Saturday mornings – and got the sack. The little magazine I produced for the school boarding house, with great satisfaction, I gave up – to dedicate myself to science. But these were as nothing compared with a sudden, great burden.

Once relations with the current lady began to wither,

Jim began to cast around for a successor. Somebody younger, if possible; of child-bearing age. When someone appropriate came into view, he felt the time had come for an all-out assault on his residual marriage. But Olga refused to budge – and in those days, before no-fault divorce, she was the one who had to be activated. The most that could be levelled at her was to describe her conduct, in mid-1951, as 'constructive desertion'. (A wonderful legal understatement.) So Jim decided she must be made to 'see reason'.

His instrument would be me. I would not be allowed to see her until she agreed to a divorce. The time-honoured pattern of alternating weekends would be sus-pended. If I didn't co-operate, then I would be taken away from school. Effectively that was my whole world…Since – once I turned fourteen – he had periodically threatened to do this, that being the legal minimal school-leaving age (and his), the whole situation was deeply disturb-ing. Never would he have had a clearer motive. I was not much over fifteen, and had no-one to turn to: the sympa-thetic housemaster showed little interest when I trenched on these issues – because he could see it was a domestic matter, one in which no other adult (least of all those at the school) could interfere.

Moreover, my own position had moved closer to my father's. For a couple of years I had hoped that my parents would come together again. At my aunt's guest house they met, briefly, when Jim stayed a few days; but they smiled awkwardly when I raised it. Gradually the realisation dawned on me that a reconciliation would never happen. My father's propaganda war against Olga was too unrelenting; she would just say, in her understated way, and charitably, 'He's not well...Not since the accident' (the most recent one). And as I advanced through my teens, I saw less and less point in her sustaining the myth of marriage. He had a succession of live-in lovers. Perhaps Olga might find a husband; there were men circling about, interested. In the meantime I found a way of seeing her, if only for half an hour or so, on the way back to school from my father's. After three or four months of this, no doubt moved partly by my distress, Olga agreed to divorce him.

Meanwhile the government fell – for with a well-developed sense of timing, my father became ill. He was hospitalised for a couple of months. The complaint – although I forget now what it was – was serious: they always were. It was as though he would work himself up into a lather, and at the moment you were most exasperated with him, you would have to go as a penitent to his medically endorsed bedside. The unreasonableness, his probable exhaustion and the culminating illness, always seemed to come as a package. That bed became the bunker. The 'accident' of 1934 had taught him how effectively he could play for sympathy from hospital – as Olga had found to her cost.

Often the recovery was equally sudden. And so it was this time. Within a year — despite a last-minute jibbing from Olga, reluctant to sign the papers that would make the divorce absolute — he had found a new house and a new wife, with prospects of a new life. Amidst all this, the piffling matter of my doing humanities was conceded.

I attended the marriage ceremony, but don't remember where it was.

II

A challenge beyond bearing

We do not seem to breed that type in Australia.

Dame Nellie Melba

I MUST HAVE BEEN ELEVEN – GAZING AT THE EMPTY OVAL from the monkey bars – when I realised that I could not be complete anywhere. Not at school, which by common consent among boarders was a 'concentration camp'. (Boys ran away, and were sometimes brought back by the police.) Nor at my father's place, since he was strict and unpredictable; nor even at my mother's, which was so relaxed and indulgent I knew it to be only a respite. But there was, in fact, a fourth side to the quadrilateral, one which confirmed the pattern already established to make me a natural sojourner.

Cloverlea farm was a magical place, situated right on the sea: only the single-track railway and the coast road lay between them. (There was so little traffic in those days that playmates would naughtily sunbake on the highway.) Woody Hill rose up behind, to some one hundred metres; the property extended, past a generous sprinkling of gums, to the summit. From the far corner you could see the cone of St Valentine's Peak, a smaller, rough-hewn Fuji. Closer to the house was the pitted home paddock, made so by generations of cows coming in to be milked; twilight at Cloverlea was calibrated by the put-put-put of the milking machine, and the bleak, distracted call of plovers. Just beyond was the first of the sheep-filled paddocks, lined with ti-tree. Further on could be found the palings of an old ruined house (a 1917 calendar still on a wall), and then an enchanting glade, with fern trees. A little stream ambled past. It ran almost entirely within the property, and was known to contain platypus. Although they are more common in Tasmania, I never saw one.

Perhaps that was partly because I spent a lot of time in the house. It was nothing much to look at: a weatherboard Edwardian, it faced a large, overgrown garden, with shrubs ranged around fruit trees. Inside, a long room at the back served as both kitchen (containing the warm Aga stove) and dining room: in wet weather, Gwen would quietly prepare a meal, head down over a bowl while all the kids would hurtle past. The doors had been opened for us, so on we would rush, past the old telephone fixed to the wall, around to the front veranda, through Cec's sombre bedroom (linoleum and wood panelling) and so past the kitchen again. It was a characteristically sensible move: all energies spent, we were quite tractable after that.

In the front of the house was the lounge, where we would retreat after the evening meal. In front of the fire I learned to play Monopoly; but in that room I learned much else. The generous bookshelves were well stocked, and – like the room – frozen at the turn of the twentieth century. That only added to its appeal. I tackled the massive volumes of the *Waverley Novels*, but didn't get very far. On the other hand, four huge illustrated volumes on the Boer War were endlessly fascinating, since I was now aware of my family's South African connection. But history here was not static: the past was closer to the surface.

I was struck by the way people, over afternoon tea, would sometimes talk of pioneers, or even of the 'blacks', convicts and bushrangers of the older Tasmania, that beyond Latrobe. One day I walked in to tea (and Anzac biscuits) and there on the table were a couple of mounted, sepia photographs, of a local landscape and another family house. There had been Mackenzies along this strip of coast for a hundred years already. And then one day, fossicking in a drawer (as they were quite content for me to do), amongst assorted clothing I came across an old envelope. It was addressed to some relatives, at 'Table Cape, Van Diemen's Land'. I was twelve, but even so, the philatelic pull of its Cape of Good Hope triangular stamp (a rarity) instantly slackened. Van Diemen's Land really existed! And Table Cape could be seen from the point, only a few minutes' walk away! I picked up the force of the continuity, represented by the object held in my hand. It was an epiphany, helping to propel me into a lifetime's dedication to history.

Tasmania felt like another country; as a television documentary styled it in 1964, 'Not Quite Australia'. There was the arrestingly named (particularly for a child) Tasmanian Devil, plus the persistent claims people made to have sighted the thylacine. The Tasmanian emu (already gone) had been smaller; kookaburras were not native to the island, but introduced relatively recently. And the people loved the place, relishing its uniqueness. A family living in another house on the farm would, after dinner, occasionally play a special parlour game: going through the alphabet, finding for each letter the name of a Tasmanian river this time, or a mountain the next.

Living at Cloverlea were brother, sister – called by me 'Uncle Bob' and 'Auntie Gwen', as was customary then – and a cousin, Cec. Bob – addressed by my father on a Christmas card envelope as 'The Laird, Clan Mackenzie' – was stocky, thoughtful, and calm in temperament – the antithesis of his old friend Jim, which may have been part of the reason they got on so well. His conversation exhibited sound judgement, for he had both the conservative temperament and the openness often found in intelligent farmers. He was a Liberal (the default middle-class position, under Menzies) who would say of the Labor premier, 'I vote for Eric Reece, because I consider him good for Tasmania!' His table talk was rarely without a ripple of humour. But on the rare occasions he was annoyed, he could show ferocity. Gwen, his sister (and Jim's former girlfriend) could let out unexpected gales of laughter, and while she did not seem to care much for tots, she was very kind to a small boy, and then the teenager, and then the man. As the years rolled on, I realised that our common experience of Jim – and distrust of him – became a bond. ('I consider him Public Enemy Number One!' she declared.) While she later married, she had no children; at times it felt as though I was the son she might have had by him.

Across the way, and eventually the hub of a nursery, was a new weatherboard house where lived Auntie Maud. Maud was a little girl when the Cooper family arrived at Emu Bay in 1892. She was a keen stamp collector, with many stamps stretching back to Queen Victoria's reign; she also had albums of old postcards – which intrigued me for their exoticism and quality coloured printing. Maud was intensely practical. Although she had been keen on a young man who lost his life after volunteering for the Boer War (hence the volumes) she decided to dress like a man – trousers, heavy gumboots, and short, cropped hair. She had renounced femaleness as surely as an Albanian 'sworn virgin'. Only precision remained of her English accent; hers was quick, curt talk. She also showed a remarkable talent for improvisation. This led to a bright idea. Since Burnie people were dumping cats that she ended up rescuing and feeding, she decided to put them to work. Blackbirds were a problem, and so visitors to the extensive strawberry beds were surprised to find, at the end of 1953, that she had chained up cats to patrol them. Long before there were cat-flaps, she had holes put in at the bottom of shed doors, looking rather like square mouseholes. But the experiment must have been a failure, because when next I visited the cats had gone.

Looking back, to the stage when a family lunch was always held at Auntie Maud's, the thing that is striking is the pleasure they took in each other's company. To begin there'd be an episode of *Blue Hills* on the radio – their equivalent of a hymn to start school assembly – and then a great deal of laughter, some of it about very little. So unlike Jim's table, where all the stories were about himself. ('Daru', as Garry would later call them, after the place which figured prominently in the New Guinea ones.) The Mackenzie Coopers were unobtrusively kind, by instinct. When, years before, Jim thanked Bob and Gwen's mother for having let him stay a couple of months, she said briefly, 'That's all right...Pass it on!' (To his credit, in a measure he did – often inviting a solitary to share Christmas dinner.) Two or three times ageing bachelors came to Cloverlea to stay, and stayed on. The family had an innate sense of the worth of all human beings.

Tasmania had, in Jim's eyes, been an expedient; it might be good for me, but it would also keep me out of Olga's clutches. So from the age of nine I was sent there by myself: Wynyard airport was handy, and I could be met. Jim came occasionally, but the one who repeatedly went back was me. Whenever I wanted to visit, I could; a stay was never refused, or postponed. This kept up until the family fragmented, and even after. Small wonder that, should I be driving along that coast, it still has something of the feel of a homecoming.

FOR A TIME MY FATHER SHARED HIS HOUSE AT MONASH Avenue with tenants: sometimes we clambered over each other in the kitchen. Perhaps that was part of the reason why I saw little of his women – the private eye saw more of Claire than I did. Jim was still playing the field. Once when he called to pick me up with a friend from school, the boy said, 'I don't like the way your dad was looking at my mum' – two or three times. I wasn't aware of anything, but this was in St Kilda, and he was more worldly than me. The lady was an alluring Maori – a honeytrap for Jim.

At the beginning of 1954 any wall that existed was suddenly breached when I was suspected of having polio. I was carried off from Mentone not to the care of my mother, but to a flat in East Kew, belonging to 'Auntie Mel'. I scarcely knew her, and she didn't seem to know quite what to do with me: the custody of an eleven-year-old, however short term, was not what she had bargained for. Mel was a pleasant woman, partly Chinese, slightly distracted in manner: she would turn suddenly when being spoken to, as if tuning in. She had an antique shop – a rather good one – which innocently gloried in the name The Gay Pavilion. And she was quite devout: Jim went to Mass with her once, and was a bit shocked by all the attendant devotions, the way she crossed herself. After twelve months or so they drifted apart.

When Jim returned from a trip to New Guinea early in 1956, he brandished a photo of a rather striking woman with a fixed expression, flaunting a cigarette holder as she stood with two greyhounds circling round. 'This is Margaret', announced Jim, 'and she is going to come and live here'. I was doubly surprised, first by the announcement and then by the declaratory nature of the photograph. Margaret came. She turned out to have been a country girl from Wagga, quite without side, except when she deliberately assumed it. I didn't quite see that then, being struck instead by the fact that she had lived in London, and that with the friend who came to visit exchanged stories of bus conductors – with their accents – shouting out the names of the stops. Such enviable familiarity with the Empire city! Margaret didn't want to be 'auntied'; instead, she was a mate. Inclined to reticence, and hesitant, she was warm, sympathetic and generous. She asked her sister to send me postcards from Bruthen, which she was only too happy to do.

In fact Margaret's self-confidence was not great. For a time she loved Jim, and was prepared to run a little tuckshop for him in run-down Richmond, making sandwiches for the state school kids opposite. She was tending another of his investments. It must have been quite a comedown for someone who had lorded it (so to speak) in New Guinea. Suddenly she became quiet and withdrawn. For she had to put up with Jim's constant criticism; nothing was ever good enough, or done the right way. I suspect she increasingly took to drink.

After some twelve months the time came when, visiting Monash Avenue, I found Margaret no longer there. She had moved out, I was told. A week or two later my father and I went to see her. She had rented a room in an old mansion in Williams Road; I was shocked by the scanty furniture, and the inserted bathroom with unpainted three-ply walls. She had been discarded. Margaret wanted me to visit her, but that wasn't easy, given that I was in boarding school. Besides, I sensed Jim's disapproval. That I didn't find a way is a matter of regret to me now.

I don't remember quite how Jess appeared, partly because her ambience was Melbourne's grand old hotels, such as Scott's and the Windsor. It was my first glimpse of this world, to which she would resort at every opportunity. Jess was a member of the Western Australian squattocracy, and her closest friend was the son of a famous archbishop. When she moved into Monash Avenue, she brought her books with her – as many as Jim's, I noted at the time, but a rather superior, literary lot. She had taste, but in the manner of her caste, was not highly educated, once describing people dabbling in finding a workable philosophy of life as 'anthropologists'.

Jess was probably a little older than Jim, and, before her lips became pursed, would have had good features and almond eyes. She was capable of a wan smile, but spoke in a subdued fashion in a rather unvaried tone. Jess had been too knocked about by life to have anything but a reduced, general pessimism. In politics it was the same: she supported Moral Re-Armament, and subscribed to a right-wing information service, *Intelligence Digest*, whose crinkly airmail paper emphasised the privileged nature of its contents, as it monitored the activities of international Communism.

Jess threw herself into the relationship whole-heartedly, and sold her farming property near Albany. I was sent over – a marvellous experience for a boy not yet fifteen, with four nights on the trains – to join her former manager as he drove Jess's car to Melbourne. But like her dog Yum-Yum – who would gazump our Terry by sitting in his box with paws raised and dangling over the edge – Jess was a little too grand for Jim. He went along to the theatre, but not keenly; I probably didn't help by saying of one play, '*Janus* was anus'.

She became attached to me, nonetheless. And when they parted, Jess told me how she had made provision in her will for me to receive some income. She must have told Jim this; but when I asked a couple of times where I could get in touch with her, he showed a complete dis-inclination to tell me anything. (Perhaps he was jealous.) I imagine he dumped her mainly because he realised she would be unable to produce children; and he still wanted a second family, if only Olga would divorce him. I also suspect they parted on bad terms, and that Jess gave as good as she got. She would not be crushed like poor

Margaret. At any rate she slipped from view, and any prospect of my being a beneficiary of her will, wilted.

TO REACH MY MOTHER'S I HAD TO CATCH A TRAIN TO Toorak station. It was a misnomer: a big wooden foot-bridge over railway yards delivered you efficiently to Orrong Road. Olga was now living nearby, occupying with Tasma their parents' old house in Armadale, as they called it. Just down the road was Grandview Grove, run-ning along a ridge; its line of Victorian mansions high above Prahran spurned even the view towards the Bay. It formed a natural boundary. But the post office thought otherwise – and certainly, with subdivisions and the partition of old houses into flats, the grandeur was slip-ping away. There must have been other recalcitrants, for sometimes mail would arrive at Wynnstay Road rubber-stamped – 'Your correct postal address is not Armadale, but East Prahran, S.1.'

At Mt Eliza Olga had not been a churchgoer. But after the crisis of 1951, she began to seek the comfort of reli-gion, and the strength that faith might give her. Laura, her sister-in-law, had tried to interest her in Christian Science: Olga was acquiescent, but could never summon up much enthusiasm for its homespun meditations. For a short time she even considered the Catholicism of her Tiernan relatives, but rather more quickly decided it was not for her. She had had enough of dogmatism and male authority, and may also have not been treated as kindly as she should have been, as a deserted wife. (Another churchman, the Methodist Sir Clarence Irving Benson, around this time declined to employ her as a secretary, using the excuse that she might find that her family needed her.) Nor did Olga care for the Anglican pomposities on offer up the street, and, as often happened in those days, shopped around for a more congenial Protestant clergyman. She found him at some little distance in Armadale (proper), at the Presbyterian church, and so found her way back to the faith of her mothers.

Olga was hopeless in argument. Instead, she'd often quote the Golden Rule – 'Do unto others as you would have others do unto you' – expecting people would follow it, as a matter of course. Her unobtrusive strength of character came partly from a resumed Christianity, but even more from a sense that, for all the reverses experienced, the world was basically a benign place. You could say she was blighted by her own better instincts. She was inclined to be stoically silent about her own needs, while being solicitous for those she loved – in particular her father, and her son. Once she told me, when I was overseas, that she had written a letter she had thought self-pitying, unfair to burden me with, and so had torn it up. She then wrote another. 'On with the motley, the paint and the powder', she would say, quoting the doleful clown in *Pagliacci*: the show must go on. But because she strove hard to make the best of things, she had a strong sense of her real worth. Unlike her sister Tas, the cellist – who always had a little of the stranded public figure about her – when Olga eventually did lapse into quiet resignation, she retained a sense of dignity.

But what if another path had been taken? The last year I lived with her she told me of a man who rang and said, 'I'd like to *do* you…Mrs Davidson'. She was a bit shocked; to my surprise, also a little mesmerised. But at the first opportunity she dropped 'Mrs' from the telephone book listing. Yet there were moments when she assumed a sudden look of sadness, as if aware of what she had missed out on in life. The real problem was that she really wasn't prepared to submit herself to a male partner again. Olga just wanted a pal. Her love for Jim had been an error of compassion: not that she would ever have thought of it like that. In a corner of her heart she still loved him, or the memory of him.

Humour was her salve, together with a well-developed sense of absurdity. She would take off Jim and his bad temper. He sounded just like Donald Duck, she said – so 'Donald' he became. And she would burlesque machismo: if you said something she disagreed with, she would suddenly pull back her right arm and assume a hostile expression, as if about to clock you one. But confrontation was the last thing she wanted. If there was a bit of tension, after having stated her position quite firmly, she would immediately undercut it by moving away doing one of her father's funny walks. The sharp contrast always produced the desired laughter.

Wynnstay Road began to need a lot of attention – it was a wooden building dating from the 1880s. Not yet sixteen, I was prompting Olga to move, and events were gathering towards the divorce. Perhaps she herself felt the need for a new start, with a home chosen by herself. An early candidate was a neat, white weatherboard house in Hawksburn: to my surprise she did not seem to register that it stood right next to a major railway line. And then she lighted on a house further out, in a nondescript area that was municipally Malvern, postally Glen Iris, and adjacent to the Tooronga station. Number 63 Edgar Street (North) was a rambling Federation-style house, on a full quarter-acre block: at the back there was a privet hedge dividing a lawn from a small orchard. The trees obscured the fact that there was a factory at the bottom of the garden. We would soon become aware, with thuds that were not always dull, that from twenty to eight in the morning till four in the afternoon, metal workers were busy producing cylinders. At the front, though, the house presented well: a set-square-shaped veranda loomed over the gate, its corner setting off an attractive casement window. My father, dropping me there for the first time, took one look and said, 'Langi!' It reminded him, and no doubt Olga, of her old home.

The veranda and the adjacent lounge, done up in tasteful leaf-green, mauve and white – colours of the thirties, her best decade – became Olga's pride and joy. Occasionally she would entertain there, carefully choosing weekends. Once, though, mindful of the need to return hospitality to some rather grand ladies associated with the church, it was necessary to fall in with their schedule and invite them to come one weekday afternoon. Whatever was she going to do about the factory? So round she went to talk to the men. They must have smiled as this old duck offered them £5 (a substantial sum) to keep quiet for a couple of hours, while she held her tea party. But she must have made the request so good-naturedly, with a humorous gesture or two, that they were prepared to fall in with it. Olga had a very Australian belief in 'being natural', and could project it. On the appointed day, they held back – until one warning bang sounded a short time before they resumed work. Dexterously, Olga brought the gathering to a brisk end.

Apart from a supportive woman who lived nearby – whose sour disposition would lift when exposed to Olga's vivacity – she had no friends in the area. Instead there was family: I would stay every second weekend, while my aunt Norma and her third husband, Ern Pettifer – a name once well known, as it was up in lights when his band played at St Kilda's Palais de Danse – also visited. And then there was Tasma.

Olga's other little sister was struggling. Some time in the late forties she had been diagnosed with TB; while she recovered, all youthfulness of spirit had gone. Tasma did not take to middle age well: her primary characteristics of being open, impulsive, and a little naïve – once quite attractive – now worked against her. In conversation she tended to blurt things out, in a little crescendo of her own. But sometimes she got things spectacularly right. One day, when they came up in conversation, she bluntly stated that she didn't like cats. 'Why not, Tas?' I asked. 'Because…because they're always jumping off the table when you come into the room.'

Olga had found Tas, with her depressive moods, difficult to live with; at the same time, Tasma's bohemianism propelled her towards St Kilda – the nearest thing Melbourne then had to the inner-city life in London she had known. (It was 'cosmopolitan'.) So Tasma moved out from Wynnstay Road to a 'private hotel' (a better-than-average boarding house). After a spell, for one reason or another, she would always move on to another one. Music was her anchor, but the tragedy that threatens all performers overtook her. She remained in the orchestra, but after her illness, was no longer first cellist; then, after re-auditioning, lost her place in it. Olga meanwhile was coping with the death throes of her marriage. For a time Tas would play in the occasional 'Music for the People' concerts in the gardens, or the new Myer

Music Bowl; but eventually that stopped, too. She was desperate.

At this stage Tas received the attentions of another boarding-house inmate. Harvey had no interest in music, no conversation to speak of, and was no beau. But he was aware that she had some money, and was needy. So he decided to go for it. It was the second time Tasma would abscond to the registry office; Olga, cast by Tas as 'Girlie', was the authority figure now. She was aghast, for this time Tasma did it. The marriage fell apart within a fortnight.

Even so, Tasma would always remain Mrs Harvey Carroll — as a statement of independence, if not fulfil-ment. But Olga saw the episode for what it was — a cry for help. She was aware of Tas's deep unhappiness, and accepted the big-sister role of propping her up as much as she could. So she got used to Tasma turning up at any time, without luggage. Tas would then occupy the other twin bed in her room, and help herself to Olga's clothes and toiletries. This would last for about a week, until Olga could bear it no more. Then Tasma's camping expedition would be brought to an end. Until the next.

When together they would sit and talk a good deal of the time, one inexhaustible topic being the abdication crisis of 1936. The two of them had been around twenty when that heart-throb the Prince of Wales came to Aus-tralia, and no doubt they had been caught up in the general excitement. Now they continued to ponder the brazenness of Mrs Simpson, the most unlikely person (they thought) to capture the heart of a king. Then they might get up from the kitchen table, the favoured site of these discourses, and go into Olga's best room for some music. On the piano Olga would accompany her sister. A favourite was Saint-Saëns' *The Swan*; a swansong for them both.

Olga was not intellectual. In reading, as in music, her tastes were middlebrow: the novels that enthused her were *Desirée, My Brother Jack,* and *The Shoes of the Fisherman*. The *Herald* office had offered her this culture in daily instalments. She was comfortable with it, did not presume to venture beyond – indeed she would later write to me of somebody being 'quite intelligent, for a woman'.

As any hope of financial rescue from bachelor Tiernan uncles gradually expired with each one of them, Olga realised that she would have to come to terms with Jim. But the divorce settlement was meagre; she therefore let half the house. Reactively proud and self-reliant, she kept on working – her typing so good that strangers commented on its excellence. But the hours grew shorter, and the gaps between jobs longer. Olga held out against taking the pension until she was sixty-four, when she was persuaded to do so by her sister Norma, who had no such qualms.

At seventy Olga could pass for being not much over fifty. But she was running on empty, almost. An old trick of hers, when she felt down, was to go quietly to the piano, play a few notes on the keyboard, then allow a slow, sad

tune to emerge, then another, and another, till eventually she was playing a quite sprightly one. In this way she
would turn her mood round, and eventually close the lid
and rise from the piano quite brightened up.

Even so, there was a long diminuendo. Olga's scrap-
book had stopped early in her marriage. There had been
practically no new photographs since 1945, for – with
too great a consciousness of what she had once looked
like – she would do all she could to avoid the camera. As
the 1960s moved on, visitors declined, deaths increased,
phone conversations lengthened and then fell away.

Not surprisingly, Olga clung to the past. She was
inclined to keep things because they had always been
there. It never crossed her mind that the heavy Edwardian
furniture in the 'Blue Room' at Edgar Street was wrong for
the young couple in their twenties to whom it was let.
On a nearby stand a fine brass pot proffered a long-dead
shoot. Olga's mental grid became almost unchanging. She
remained loyal to the *Herald*, and insisted on wearing a fox
fur to the opera, despite my suggestion it would be dramatically out of fashion. She coped with decimal currency
– just – but never quite mastered how to write a dollar
sign. And when I mentioned somebody, she might say
that she had known someone with that name, and then
ask, 'I wonder if they're related?' Not a foolish question,
in the Melbourne she grew up in, which totalled only half
a million people. But another matter altogether in a city

four times that size, as it had become in the late 1960s. The present would often steal a march on her, but she took precautions. Olga's kitchen clock was slowly running down, so whenever she thought of it, she'd cheerily give it a winding boost. The result was that, when staying with her, I would always just miss the train before the one I was going for.

Some months before I left for South Africa in 1967, Jim suddenly expressed some concern about her, living in that big, ageing, weatherboard house, on such a huge block. Shortly after, he was dropping me off at Edgar Street with some luggage, when suddenly Olga appeared, smartly dressed in black. 'Hello, Jim', she said warmly. Her dress indicated there was nothing casual about this encounter: she had glimpsed a small boy running about on his previous call. Jim was invited in; the conversation was surprisingly relaxed. When I sailed away, he told me he would keep an eye on her, and the house. I was pleased, not least by the measure of reconciliation.

But some months later an aerogramme turned up, with surprising contents. One day he had gone over to see Olga. Perhaps assuming too much, regarding her place as a regular port of call, Jim touched a nerve which she didn't know she had: she must have turned on him, told him to clear out. At the very least she drew on a strength that was new to him. Eve, his second wife, said he came back saying, 'I fear for my life!' There may even have been talk of a knife. Given previous melodramas, that could be put aside: it would have been too violently out of character. Nevertheless, something happened. Jim claimed it gave him a heart attack. A few months later, when I returned to Melbourne, he would drive me over occasionally – but when he did, he always stopped a little short of Edgar Street itself. Curiously, when I asked my mother about this incident, she would not talk about it. That was uncharacteristic as well.

However, Olga's attitude towards me remained unchanged – indeed, it did not modulate or develop as it might have done. Apart from early childhood, we were probably closest when I was about sixteen: I can see her now, marching down the passage to a jaunty orchestral record I was playing. I was just young enough then to move uncritically into much of her world – prompted to do so after being deprived of access to her by my father. But tensions soon arose: as I slowly moved towards rejecting religion, Olga was hurt by the way I was increasingly uncomfortable in accompanying her to church. She might have nodded ruefully had she heard Edna Everage's formulation: 'It's a pity they have to grow up!'

Because her love was so strong, her sense of identification with me was complete. The corollary was an expected congruency of assumptions and attitudes. When I said something she didn't like, she might, in a semi-comic turn, slowly say, 'To his mother!' That soon drew the retort, 'To hi' smother!' The night before I left for England in 1969, Olga arranged a little farewell gathering of relatives and contemporaries; she couldn't understand that at a certain point I might want to disappear to be with someone special.

I was her ideal companion. Male, but unthreatening, hopefully unchallenging: a diminutive version of Jim. Just how much so would come to alarm me. A day or two after I returned, she came into my room and addressed me as if I were my father. I can see it, now: I sported a beard, and was not, in many ways, the person who had left for England three years before. The end of absence, too, had stirred up vivid memories in her. I had already concluded that adult sons living with their mothers can be disastrous: the mothers tend to want to make husbands of them.

Yet in the important things Olga was not possessive. That I should go overseas for six years in all was accepted, without demur – even though she realised (more fully than I did) that it would create difficulties for her. And she kept referring to my 'getting a girl', although when one rang she would complain about the length of the phone calls, or think her 'forward'. Later, when I was in London, she accepted what she saw as the prospect of a girlfriend with equanimity – 'it's time you had one anyway'. Alone and older than most mothers with children my age, she was perhaps less jealous than anxious and insecure.

Returning from England, I decided I should tell her I was gay. As quick as a flash came the immortal response, 'But dear, what about the police?' Olga was instantly on my side: what are we going to do? But gradually, since she was beginning to fail, respectability reasserted itself from the default position afforded by social norms. Passing references to girlfriends would be made again. Gently I would repeat my disclosure, only a few days later to be girled again. After a week or so I realised – with some pain at the separation of destinies – that it would be kinder to just give up.

BUT TO RETURN TO THE 1950S. AT MOUNT ELIZA THERE seemed to be no playmates around my own age, while my solitariness was underscored by the sombre household: my mother was often thoughtful and preoccupied, even during the week when my father was absent. At Frankston State – a good walk and a bus ride away – I got on well enough with the other kids, but their mothers! They seemed so young! Sometimes I was subjected to bullying. One day (to the surprise of us both) I punched the worst offender on the nose. Blooded, he became my first friend.

Mentone Grammar, where I would spend nine years, was very different. It was twenty-four/seven: a total environment. Bullying there was inescapable: there were times when, unlike day boys, you did not see the mas-

ters as imposing discipline so much as guaranteeing pro-
tection. Once they disappeared, anything could happen.
The boys left in charge as captains or vice-captains could
be the worst oppressors, and not only in the capricious
way they wielded a punishing sandshoe. Once one of
them came up to my bunk, looked at me eye to eye, then
spat in my face before silently moving away. On another
occasion, when everyone was stirring well before we were
officially woken at seven, I was told to get out of bed by
two older boys. I was to 'run the gauntlet'. There wasn't
much of an explanation. Others began to slither out of
their bunks, and proceeded to twist and knot their towels.
I would have to run around the single beds that lay in
the centre of the dorm, hands covering my face and head
as best I could, copping it sweet. The comics are right, I
noted with surprise: you really do see stars.

Not long afterwards the Principal, on one of his
nightly jaunts with his torch (checking to see that everybody was there) heard the sudden patter of thirty pairs of
feet as boys suddenly made for their beds. He had inter-
rupted one of these events. He soon elicited what had
been going on – 'Initiations, sir'. But instead of immediately exerting authority and imposing a penalty, he began
to discourse on initiations as part of tradition. 'Manners
maketh man', he parroted: traditions had to be respected.
To the amazement of us all, he waved his torch and said,
'Continue!' The boys could scarcely believe their ears.

They were slow to leave their beds, but gradually the two rows reassembled; while the blows were tokenistic at first, they soon found form. I remember feeling – for I couldn't quite articulate it – that (drawn from history though it was) this statement effectively endorsed mob rule. There was no safety anywhere.

In class it was better. I soon distinguished myself in geography and history: in loneliness at Mt Eliza I had pored over maps, and knew the capitals even of West Indian islands. Displaying such knowledge – hand up most of the time – must have been tedious for the other boys, but one way or another we were all into display. I always hovered around the top of the class, never making it to no. 1, but the school found a way to give me a prize each year. One year it was for divinity (which delighted my mother), given on the strength of vividly written answers in the exam.

The masters were on the whole kindly. John Anwyl, a real live socialist, was not particularly so; he was better – provocative, humorous, encouraging. But living at the place, and having a fragmented family background, meant that I didn't always make a clear distinction between a specific task, and functionally involving myself with others to complete it – and the general social context. At fourteen, after some weekend cadet session, I went up to the Regular Army sergeant looking for some conversation, some hint of personality. It got nowhere. I learned my lesson, and eighteen months later at cadet camp kept my head down before another Regular Army sergeant. It was just as well. One lad was a little slow, and dreamy. 'Where do you think you are, sonny?' bawled the sergeant. 'St Paul's ca-fuckin'-thedral?'

The school's ideology was sub-imperial: Australia was just taken for granted. Years later I discovered that the Principal's uncle had been a chaplain to the King; that sustained his Britishry. But there were also a core of imperial auxiliaries – Seventh Day Adventists from New Zealand. The worst offender was the music master, who taught us not only 'Land of Hope and Glory' but a number of lesser imperial anthems, together with spiritless English folksongs. He also played, when I was thirteen, a recording of parts of Handel's *Water Music* – and then dictated notes on the esoteric dance the bourrée. Just what Melbourne teenage boys needed!

Ten years after leaving school, I came across a contemporary in the street. As he drew away, he turned round and said, 'It was imperialist...wasn't it?' It was, in all sorts of ways. For stamp collectors, since Australian ones were dull and infrequent, 'British Empire only' had the cachet – 'prestige', to use a favourite imperial word. (We didn't realise it, but stamp collecting was imperialism in lowest gear.) For over six months in 1953–54, the royals were hardly out of the papers: the Queen's coronation was followed by the first Australian tour by a reigning monarch. Buying sweets, you drew away from the tuck shop to find a card of a king or queen of England inserted between you and the toffee. It was the era of pimples, short pants, and coronations. A school pageant at this time included a chorus, 'Cheer, boys, cheer, cheer for our Indian Empire!' At Mentone Grammar no-one seemed aware that it had been happily defunct for six years.

A Mentone education in those days was pretty rackety: many of those who went over the top at the Matriculation exam, having been cossetted by internal ones to that point, were mown down by the external markers. Quite undeterred, the Headmaster, a keenly sympathetic man with a great sense of theatre, would tell us in assemblies how proud he was to be associated with a school such as this. The comparison, drawn not too subtly, was with 'state school boys'. Pure snobbery: they probably had a better education.

'He tries at sport, too!' the Headmaster optimistically noted on one report. But I had neither talent nor liking for it. Now that sport has become compulsory for the whole country, I can claim that my resistance movement goes back to the mid-1950s. (In football I find the best way to maintain this position is to barrack for whoever Carlton happens to be playing at the moment – that way I combine consistency with variety.) Occasionally the Principal would come to my rescue by requiring me to do some chore when the sport periods began. Otherwise out on the field I went, bored shitless by cricket until the ball came hurtling towards me like a meteorite. The only sensible thing to do was to stand aside.

I was aware that I seemed different, but had no real sense of its basis. There was some sexual activity among boarders, but it co-existed with lots of talk about sheilas and showing each other pictures of women in sexy poses. What some of us did with each other wasn't *real* sex – any more than what he did with Monica Lewinsky was for Bill Clinton. And in one sense this was right – 'just a stage'. It no more affected the course of most boys' sexual history than spasmodic homosexuality shaped the long-term preferences of adult males incarcerated in single-sex institutions.

Other senses of difference were real enough. Although my nickname recognised my interest in geography, it was history that fascinated me more. I loved looking at old books, maps, and photographs, seeking connection with the past. When eight or nine I tried to write a mythical neo-Aboriginal history of Mt Eliza, but soon realised it all had to be made up. Around this time I discovered a pre–First World War atlas someone had thrown out: the different boundaries and different colours (purple for a vanished German colonial empire) I found riveting, for their strong sense of past normalcies. A little later, some segments of the heavily illustrated *Picturesque Atlas of Australasia*, found at the school fete, were even more exciting, as they included views of Melbourne as it had been in the 1880s. By the time I left school, I had some feeling that while advancing forward, delving into the past would enrich experience, and in a vicarious way increase it: the present became a hinge.

I wanted to be away from the here and now: from the grey sandy soil of Mentone, the grey skies, the grey uniform, wandering around in the hours after school – you were allowed to venture out of the school grounds only once a week – half-starved and bored. The historical dimension promised a double exoticism.

MEANWHILE MY FATHER WOULD SOMETIMES THREATEN that since I was now fourteen – in 1956 still the minimum school leaving age – I should go out and work (as he had done). But then I won a scholarship, a hefty sum of money, after writing an account of a visit to an oil refinery. It was, of course, paid to the parents: generously he gave me ten pounds of it. Subsequently I went to Tasmania, made a beeline for the oldest bookshop in Launceston, and spent it all on Tasmanian books. My father didn't know what to think. On the one hand it showed a strong, clear, commendable interest; on the other...books (and booklets)! Frittered away! He did not realise the half of it. That year I had scrimped and saved, and sometimes been quite inventive; but I found that the economic imperative flattened out everything else in the world, denying it autonomy. I would never allow this to happen again.

My father was well aware that I seemed to be developing different values: I needed to be brought under closer control. That would be secured by my becoming a day boy, from Monash Avenue. A conversation was held with the Headmaster of a nearby grammar school, but nothing came of it. Perhaps the woman of the day put her foot down.

I think I was a genuine puzzle to him. Any adult I came into contact with was likely to be asked (it was always a he) what he thought of me. Bob Mackenzie, when requested, submitted a written report: he had the grace to show it to me. There I read the perceptive judgement that nothing was too much trouble for anything I cared about. Beyond that, there was a constant sense of having to mind my p's and q's. I was always getting into trouble for saying things I hadn't quite said, often to people with whom I thought you could be unguarded. I remember thinking, returning to Mentone for the new school year, that I was being brought closer to the time when I would have to endure this no longer. I wrote in a textbook: '23rd July, 1963 [when I turned twenty-one] – Independence Day!'

At this time I was visiting my mother one week-end, my father the next. (Christmas was split down the middle.) This exposed me to their different plaints, or in my father's case, rants: he wanted a divorce, and Olga was denying him one. Although I did not realise it then, it was a kind of apprenticeship in becoming an historian: learning that contradictory truths could exist side by side, along with exaggerations and falsehoods, and that – gradually – one must learn to make one's own judgement. But there were two more immediate effects.

One was that, as the divorce crisis gathered, I found escape in music. I had always had a considerable aptitude for it – in first grade it was the only glimmer of hope for me – but my father overruled the possibility of piano lessons, or anything else. His constant beef was that the school did not have a gymnasium. Then, when I was fifteen, I heard a radio serial on the lives of Gilbert and Sullivan. Unusually, it included the songs *sung*, since the D'Oyly Carte Company in England then rigorously controlled the copyright. Many of the tunes had been familiar to me since childhood, thanks to a wind-up gramophone. But this was a revelation. It was not only the wide variety of tunes, but the sparkling use of language – all put to comic ends. So I sang them, in public – overcoming my residual stammer. And began to whistle: like a kettle, it was a sign of distress, or at least the need for attention.

There is a Jewish saying that 'to be funny, you first have to think sad'. Soon I was writing parodies of Gilbert and Sullivan, applied to the school, and then of the musical *My Fair Lady*. Following the imperatives of satire gave me a lot of satisfaction. When there's a sense of repression, and some intelligence, wit becomes the only place where resistance can go. But there was little point: no audience. More 'successful' was the little underground paper I put out, given the mega-respectable name of *The Times*. There was only one copy, which, appearing in a 'handy subversive size', could be held secretively in the palm. These samizdats were quite absurd: they drew on Ronald Searle's send-up of a British boys' public school, but mostly – through Russianising the names of the masters – made out that the school authorities practised an inept form of Communism. It was the height of the Cold War: 'Borrie', the Principal's nickname, was given flight as the school was christened 'Borriegrad'.

Meanwhile my father began to turn his house into a fortress. Brick walls went up, the back gate fixed so that it could not be opened from the outside. A room adjacent to the washhouse became chocker with tins of food and other household goods – for some unspecified emergency. My bedroom door would be opened peremptorily at 7 am: 'Time to get up!' There was no good morning. He felt no need for politeness. 'Jim – [or Eve] – I'll get you to…'. He was always getting us to. I'd hear the call, even in my university years: 'Are you there, Jim?' I was never left alone with my books. He always felt he had the right to drag me away at any time to do a menial task.

I was pretty unsatisfactory, in his view. Not Rhodes Scholarship material at all. I was no good at boxing (the only extra lessons he paid for). I was not much good at things mechanical – a condition worsened by his inter-ruptive impatience. And he was alarmed – when I was about thirteen – by my puppy fat and sparse body hair (then). He'd examined me carefully (keep still for massa!): underlinings in a book he'd been reading showed that he was anxious he'd produced a poofter. Meanwhile he constantly exhibited road rage – getting out of the car to abuse someone at the lights. I wasn't around much, but he must have done this over a dozen times with me sit-ting there, waiting. But around 1960 it suddenly stopped: perhaps he'd been challenged, realised he was older – and didn't do it any more.

However he would still bail up a pretty young woman behind a counter, regaling her with tales of New Guinea – which she just had to put up with, since she couldn't escape. And once, in Tasmania, exasperated by my lack of interest in a girl (who was sixteen to my twelve) he pushed me in her direction. Why couldn't I be a herosexual, like him?

His friend Bob Mackenzie could calmly say, when explaining farm machinery, that these were called male and female parts, 'for obvious reasons'. It was a rare acknowledgement by an adult of the underworld of sex-uality. Around that time I had just got used to the idea of a magazine calling itself *Man* and being full of pic-tures of women. One day (he couldn't help himself) Jim sat reading it in front of me. I tittered, and was brought up sharply. It was not like that at all. With the veneer of hypocrisy he could always apply at a moment's notice, he asserted that this was ART, the beauty of the natural form, and photography. Yet around the same time the message he'd wanted me to extract from reading an autobiography by one of the Lindsays was, 'When he wanted a root he went out and got it'.

Meanwhile there were all kinds of threats, from suspect people who might be out to do the same. One day my father picked me up early from school (as he'd do, occasionally) and we went to Mentone beach. In the car was a handsome man in his thirties, from a big property in the Western District. We swam: the man, exuberant, invited me to dive and swim between his legs. He was fun: I really liked him. But my father was cool, and I never heard of the fellow again. More telling was an incident when he made a scene with a man in a milk bar. I was only eleven, doing my first holiday job at a garage over the road. The man was in his fifties, and very nice to me. 'You're being too friendly with my son!' my father threatened. There was more. And I can see the look now – so strong I half-perceived it then – not only of passivity in that man, but also of implacable hatred. Afterwards, I tried talking to him in our usual friendly way. Nothing. He had been deactivated.

Jim was scornful of the effeminate – the public school accent of one of the neighbours was caricatured so as to imply it. But then he had little patience with the feminine: he disliked women. It was always 'some little popsy', 'some floozy', or an 'old girl' (for authority figures – even when they were younger). If oppositional, then it was 'a bitch'. He had no use for the words 'woman' or 'lady'. His response to women, once they had a particular place in his network, tended to become standardised and mechanical. So any man who was smitten was dismissed as 'cuntstruck'.

My father later claimed he was influenced more by women than by men – strong mature ones, I would think, whom he would admire for their equanimity. But he was happiest, to judge by the stories he told, enjoying the male camaraderie of Queenstown or the Islands. This went a little further than the rituals of homosociality. He admired quiet-spoken, manly men (silent and intelligent) and surprised me when he once described the boxer Alan Rudkin as having the delicacy of a poet. An acceptable way of expressing light physical attraction was to describe a young fella as 'a fine cut of a lad'. Until Jim's second marriage, and even after, there was a succession of them: friends, confidants, apprentices. Earlier I had been surprised when we went on a picnic with his girlfriend Mel and her brother – who brought along a couple of stewards from a ship in port. Jim was gobsmacked by the brazenness of it, and commented even as they were there in front of us – with a touch of admiration. On another occasion we were driving on a back road in Tasmania when the car broke down. We walked up to the nearest farmhouse for some help. Coming to the door was a man of about his own age, who was a bit edgy, and behind him a younger one, who was very responsive. Again my father was more intrigued than anything.

But I was something else. I was fooling around, sexually, with the kid next door in a distant corner of the back yard when suddenly Jim appeared on the enclosed veranda. 'He'll see us', said Peter. I dismissed the idea. A hand may have lingered; 'Go on', I said. Part of me wanted him to know. My father said nothing, indeed went back inside, but there were two odd effects. The first was that for the next week he couldn't see enough of the boy next door. Then, a few weeks later, my father took me to the same corner of the backyard after some misdemeanour and pummelled me, with a pillow – ineffectively. I noticed that he was distraught; in a few minutes it was played out. I now realise he was trying to erase that visual memory, that offence, pretend it hadn't happened. But he couldn't, and in that he felt he was beaten. What he must have seen as the curse on the Davidson line – the vision of the empty house – was too strong for him.

It would have been very difficult for Jim. As a macho man, he suffered delusions of gender. And there was a perfect fit which homosexuality threatened to subvert: 'Masculinity needed to be hard and heterosexual', one historian has written, 'if it were not to succumb to the

Communist threat'. Conservative hegemony went with a general homogeneity – enlivened by a few colourful 'characters' (he being one). So my father saw himself – with a kind of back-up from base.

It is worth recalling how much conformity then was both pervasive and expected. It was a time when ethnic kids in a western suburbs school might be told, when they asked about playing soccer, that they would just have to use goal posts; their parents might be frowned upon if they spoke in their own language on public transport. Even swearing was often headed off: there were still a lot of 'darns' and 'ruddys' around – instead of damn and bloody – and 'fuckin' wasn't commonly used till the seventies. It was the era of rigid censorship, when serious novels might be banned because they might corrupt a teenage daughter. Homosexuals subverted this anodyne order; they were demonised as a secret brotherhood who were often in league with those seeking to undermine the West. In 1954, the CIA sacked forty-eight agents as 'security risks', the State Department adding another 117 officials to the list: almost half had files 'indicating sex perversion'.

One day my father put a copy of the scandal sheet *Truth* on the kitchen table – the headlines were about a disgraced MP, who had been sent to jail for soliciting in a public toilet. I was puzzled – an MP? – and this unknown, incomprehensible behaviour. If my father thought I was incipiently gay, I was well short of this realisation myself.

If displaying the paper was intended as a piece of aversion therapy, it failed utterly.

I didn't think of myself as not being 'normal' at all. But by the age of thirteen, I noticed that other boys were changing – discovering girls – and that I was not. Perhaps then it was not a matter of being 'special', but being different – something much more loaded. And perhaps – horror of horrors – this compulsion was at the heart of it. Having ambition and believing it a duty to do well, I felt – on the rare occasions I chose to think about it – somehow betrayed. I would have to control this impulse, eliminate it, and until my mid-twenties hoped that a young woman might come along who would sweep me into heterosexuality. In the meantime I would have to be on my guard.

ALTHOUGH I ENTERED MY FINAL SCHOOL YEAR WITH SOME trepidation about the world beyond – having had little experience of it – it was soon the case that the time to leave couldn't come fast enough. At the prompting of John Anwyl, I sat an examination for an Ormond College scholarship, and got one. There was no great financial benefit, but it did secure a place in a residential college at Melbourne University. My father was not keen on the idea, and insisted on coming with me to the appointment with the Acting-Master. A dignified, hawk-eyed man who emanated a sense of humanely exercised responsibility, he managed to reconcile Jim to the situation. Previously, my father had ridiculed any interest I had shown in a diplomatic career – you needed wealth and connections for that, he said. It was an image drawn from old British films, but who was I to correct him? And when I suggested law – and perhaps becoming a barrister – he ridiculed that idea too. How could a seventeen-year-old possibly aspire to be like a forty-five-year-old man in his verbal and tactical prime? He had already received some money from the Education Department to contribute towards education expenses for my final school year, and he was loath to pay it back. A teacher I had contracted to be, and that was that.

It was 1960: the last year Melbourne would be the only university in the city. The first few weeks were confusing. At Ormond there were initiations, which involved being ostracised by the existing College members and being addressed by them as 'Scum'. This kept up implacably for a fortnight. Down the path at the University proper, the teaching at the beginning of first year was in some ways perverse. In English I, we began with TS Eliot and Gerard Manley Hopkins, as a kind of test or challenge to the students. Hopkins' preciously keening, gobs-of-gossamer verse has been high on my list of dislikes ever since. History also was disappointing. A course on Early Modern Europe turned out to be a shambles. One day a middle-aged English lady appeared from nowhere and began lecturing on two cities — London and 'Be'eh'. It took me a while to realise she meant Bury, that is Bury St Edmunds. A more rigorous course was the weekly lecture in Ancient History Part I Honours, which consisted entirely of an examination of the Athenian Tribute Lists, inscribed on stone. This was altogether too advanced a course for first year; implicitly acknowledging this, the lecturer rounded out his opening performance by drily listing its academic virtues, repeating the refrain that if you weren't happy with this focus, 'then you should not be doing Ancient History Part I Honours'. There was a severe logic about that, but the problem was that if you wished to do Honours History at all, you had to do this subject. Otherwise I would have been out of that room like a shot.

I might have been intellectual, I was certainly serious and exploratory. But I was not academic — that is to say, prepared to apply myself totally to any given body of knowledge to refine technical and analytical skills. I wanted breadth. Although I would not have styled it so, then, I was searching for authenticity. With history, the further removed in place and time it was, the less I felt any connection. When I tried to make one, as in an essay on medieval European travellers going to China (an appealingly improbable connection) I was chided for not being sufficiently restrained and scholarly. The approved approach seemed too purposeful, reductive. It left out too much. As for English, it was in thrall to those misplaced

theologians, the Leavises: one had to learn to mouth critical responses almost as if in nursery school, with the name
of the Cambridge gurus inserted in place of 'Simon Says'.
No authenticity there.

My first great intellectual discovery at this time was
not at university at all. Visiting my aunt Norma and her
husband and exploring their bookshelves, I picked up
Alfred Einstein's *Music in the Romantic Era*. It was a revelation, since it linked what to that moment had been two
separate worlds: music and history. Lucidly it set forth
how Romantic opera had been a vital expression of liberal
nationalist sentiment in early-nineteenth-century Europe.
I now had a particular handbook to the world of classical
music I was just entering. The light, early Romantic idiom
of Weber and the early Wagner (*The Ring* was pretty much
unrecorded, then) was attractive to this eighteen-year-
old, optimistically setting out on self-realisation himself.

In my formal studies (until the very end) I was not
distinguished. It was not till third year that I made any
impression on my teachers, with a paper on Napoleon III
– tellingly biographical in approach. I was still quite shy.
Once I sat in a tutorial which the lecturer was scouring for
an answer; I was too afraid to speak up with what I knew.
In student activities, leftist politics appalled me with
their groupthink. I rejected an ALP that still had White
Australia in its platform, and would threaten Jim Cairns
with expulsion unless he resigned from the Immigration

Reform Group. For a short time, as friends were involved in it, I joined the Liberal Club – and voted Labor while still a member. I could find no firm base from which to exercise any satirical talent – and any pressing need for it had flown out the window on leaving Mentone. I didn't have sufficient ability to venture into student theatre. But I did become involved with *Farrago*, the student newspaper, as a result of contacts made in Ormond College.

Ormond was central to my university experience. Although an elite, single-sex institution, it was remarkably free from excluding cliques – partly because it was so effortlessly dominated by people from Scotch College that socially they were unnecessary. Moreover, the place had a liberal sprinkling of sons of the manse, children of clergymen, people familiar with the world of learning, and with a measure of austerity and making do; no snobbery there. Customarily, people stopped work at their books at ten o'clock (when the College clock also ceased to chime), and then shared a cup of coffee and biscuits with others. There was enough of a sense of community to feel that you could invite anybody. I became friendly with medical students, familiar with the boxes of bones on their desks; my closest dining companions were two lawyers, an architect, an engineer and a mathematician. Interest in classical music was a strong bond: the corridors seemed to pulsate with it. Then there was wit, and high spirits. One day, as men came into the dining hall for their customary silent breakfast, they were amazed to find a strong contingent from Women's College already in noisy possession. A day or two later the students' club came up with the perfect retort. In those days of more straitened morality – when women visiting had to be off the premises by 10 pm – the Principal of Women's College found herself billed for one hundred women, bed and breakfast.

Ormond was a formidable institution of upper-middle-class Australia, and in 1960 it was something of a time warp. Its gothic dining room had been built with Victorian conviction; past its enormous, functioning fireplaces flitted maids dressed in black, wearing aprons and lace caps. The new Master, Davis McCaughey, presided benignly even as he charmed the students' club into accepting some limitations of its powers. Doubling the size of the College, he radically changed the institution. The high table edged towards distinction. One tutor, Barry Smith, became a friend and mentor, not least for the way he epitomised the then prevailing liberal assumption: that an educated person should be as well informed as possible, on as many subjects as possible. Meanwhile university activists, often seen as a different species, actually moved *into* Ormond, availing themselves of networking opportunities. McCaughey though stressed the values of scholarship: it was Cambridge that he danced before our eyes, not England – for he was Irish. Besides – when not earthed in the wealth of the Western District – Ormond's ancient links were with Scotland. There was no conscious imperial sense about the place at all: 'Land of Hope and Glory' was never sung at College functions (unlike later). The Queen was lucky to be toasted once or twice a year.

Queens of other kinds were rarely spoken of, indeed thought about. It was customary to refer to the person you shared a study with (there were separate bedrooms) as your 'wife'. But rather than being incipiently gay, an element of ridiculousness had been pre-emptively wheeled into position – making any such relationship almost unthinkable. It did not occur to the people who did not, for various reasons, go to the College Ball, to put two and two together – for fear of making six. As it happened, years would roll by before it became apparent that of our dining group of six, four were gay. When I did come out to my closest friend, I had known him for three full years; the situation was so loaded that he did not make a similar disclosure until the next time we met.

It was a heavy number. In 1962 the progressive periodical *Nation* ran a piece attacking homosexuals, criticising a book for making 'no reference at all to the destructiveness, the masochism, the greed, envy and narcissism which will be found in varying proportion in every homosexual person'. Eagerly I awaited the next issue, to see what kind of response there would be. A letter duly appeared, answering the charges and rebutting them, soberly – but regretfully concluding that, 'for obvious reasons, I must not give you my name. "H'". There was nowhere else to go except to stay in the closet – outwardly and practically conforming, while cleaving to some secret inner truth. There was always England, one or two suggested. But even there the law had not yet been changed.

MY FATHER ADJUSTED TO MY GOING TO UNIVERSITY AND living in Ormond in his own inimitable way. He never said as much, but thought I was getting a bit above myself. Perhaps I was paying less attention to stories about head-hunters. A few months after I had begun, one of his regular visitors began to bad-mouth the Arts Faculty. The talk was so wild that I sprang to its defence, only to be silenced immediately. It was around this time, wanting to connect my two worlds, that I suggested inviting a group of friends home for a meal. No, Jim said, he didn't want his wife turned into a waitress. I tried to explore acceptable ways it might be done, but back this came like a mantra. He was hostile to any such idea. Even when a friend whose family home was nearby came over, there were difficulties. As we sat by the fire, my father was very aggressive in his questioning. The young medical student held his ground admirably – but the apology I made on walking him back to his place was received in silence.

At the same time, Jim would actively extend his presence into my new life. 'Parking the ute' near Ormond

College facilitated controlling raids. Once he came to my bedroom around eight in the morning, to find the bed unslept in. He rang Olga, of all people, full of portentous announcement. She gave it little mind; correctly, as I had slept in the study, rather than in a freezing wooden out-building, to have the benefit of a fire. Since he was lending me money on what amounted to a private HECS scheme, Jim thought Ormond was fair game. Once I found him, with a couple of people including a Maori woman he was trying to impress, walking around the ground floor showing it off. Not that he would have done a good job of it; but he hadn't even rung to arrange that we should meet. I was given a distinct sense of having disturbed them. As would become increasingly apparent, he had no respect for my territory. What was mine, was his also.

Beyond that, he would see me as being in direct competition with him. He had always been disinclined to congratulate me on any achievement, although (out of apparent earshot) he might inflict it on a visiting tradie. Now that I began to frequent second-hand booksellers, Jim wanted to come with me on these expeditions. Occasionally he did – and invariably spent ostentatiously, to show that he could. To one bookseller (a distinguished music critic) he said how 'we' (the two of them) had to keep the younger generation in their place. The man, looking at me, made no reply – I was the more regular customer, and he at once saw what I was up against. Jim did value books, but was an undisciplined autodidact. He was suspicious of more formally organised learning – it was a source of power he didn't have. Particularly when evident in his son, it must be suborned.

His view, after all was a static one: he had named me James Hector, after himself and his brother, in that order. I had been nominated for the lieutenancy. But whereas a brother may follow at a predictable pace behind, a son usually won't. He tried referring to me as 'Jim Junior', as if perpetually measuring me against the real thing. I countered this by taking a leaf from the ancient Roman Plinys, and began to call him 'James the Elder'. That did the trick.

Jim also asserted his authority in a more direct way. He had already expressed the fantasy that, when I had graduated, I might live in a caravan out the back – as a kind of useful, perpetually on call. That I could parry, allow to pass; but mowing the lawns was different. I was expected to do this once a fortnight, combining it with a weekend spent 'home'. As it happened, the History School in those days combined second-year with third-year examinations in the one session, which compounded anxieties. I wanted to be free to face up to this double-banger in my own way. When I suggested that lawn-mowing be suspended – that I might even pay for someone else to do it – the response was to break off relations totally, without any explanation. Jim was now creating a second family; he had no desire to loosen his grip on his first. He knew I was vulnerable:

an element of envy also drove him towards sabotage. Why not apply pressure when I was least able to resist it? After six weeks, relations were bumpily restored. And then, owing to a sudden vacancy, I had the chance to go on a student expedition to India. I would need some financial help; swallowing hard, my father gave it. Not to have done so might have imperilled the peace.

INDIA WAS AN EXTRAORDINARY EXPERIENCE: I REMEMBER taking in more of its pungencies with each step, as I advanced up the main staircase of the ship towards the gangplank. Once landed — and all to a Bollywood soundtrack — there was a constant parade of exuberance, desperation, minor disasters and sudden generosities. No two days were alike. In addition to the ever-present poverty, there was the high-toned idealism of the Nehru government, with its five-year-plans at home and its championing of the Third World abroad. (That had taken a knock lately, with the border war with China: but its effects were subsiding as we travelled around the country.) Meanwhile I was drawn to things like the Hindu joint family, and to the degree to which western modes had penetrated or become incorporated in Indian life. The English language was the passport — around the country, as much as to it: I remember seeing the same poster, bearing a portrait of Nehru, coming off the presses in Delhi in

the sixteen official languages. I was struck by the sophistication of the highly educated, by the elegance of West-
ernised women in their saris; people who helped make
accessible to me the ordered intricacies of Indian classical
music and Mughal miniatures. While this may now sound
a little precious, at least it wasn't as silly as the disgruntle-
ment felt by a Tasmanian university student who told me
how she was going to do a fourth-year thesis on Radhakr-
ishnan, the eminent philosopher and president of India.
He had agreed to see her, and when they met, expressed
(a puzzling) annoyance that she hadn't done any reading.

India also included a reception in the Indo-Saracenic
great hall of Bombay University – a nineteenth-century
expression of cultural fusion. Suddenly someone mentioned, in passing, that that year (1962) was the last that
Indian school-leavers would be sitting for the Cambridge
Junior Certificate. I was a little shocked. It was just dawn-
ing on me that independence was not only a change of
rulers, and opting for democracy – but would necessarily
involve a re-ordering of patterns, a different way of doing
things. Instead of an onward march of a Kennedy-style
high cultural Camelot, extending across the globe (very
much an early-sixties assumption), there might be severance, retreat. But for the moment much of it was still in
place. There was the magnificent statue of George V –
literally still the kingpin of New Delhi – and the shabby
turn-of-the-century office buildings lining the streets of

Calcutta. But – although the demise of empire had been comparable – Dalhousie Square was no Roman Forum. Any Gibbonesque feeling was more one of departure than of glory. There was no chanting of monks. That would come some years later – with the Hare Krishnas in Bourke Street.

Returning to Australia was an anti-climax. After India, Australian history seemed listless, Theory and Method a philosophical incursion into history. I decided to continue the photography I had begun in India, this time focused on Melbourne's Victorian architecture. I liked its variety, intricacy, and human scale; it spoke of other times and other values, and now often echoed ethnic voices. Meanwhile the mansions were disappearing; more than once I turned up with a companion to find the wreckers had just started on their work. About the same time, Martin Boyd's novel *The Cardboard Crown* was reprinted: dealing with Anglo-Australians, it served to people these houses. I would later laugh at its snobberies, but at that time shared some of them. More to the point, I was grateful to be given an imaginative connection to the Victorian past of the city, which up till then had been largely obscured.

Then there were the attractions of Carlton: the mix of traditional working class and Italians, together with students – some of whom (instead of sharing the general preference for a brand-new house) were beginning as young professionals to move into terrace houses and 'do them up'. In not being suburban – excoriated by Barry Humphries – there was the promise of sophistication, if not bohemianism. Carlton was already being romanticised in short stories. In 1964, my last year on an Education Department studentship, I could have bought an old bluestone cottage a minute or two from the University for £2000 ($4000): so different were the relative values, then, that it was only four or five times the value of my annual living allowance. But there were other obstacles. There was a prejudice against housing loans to buy old properties, while the government of Henry Bolte was dedicated to clearing 'the slums' of Carlton. More to the point, I wanted to be off overseas.

It was a curious time: there was a sense of nullity. One young friend brilliantly parsed 'nowhere' as 'now, here'. The long Menzies torpor continued, having just reached its crescendo with his declaring to the Queen, 'I did but see her passing by/And yet I love her till I die'. Viet Nam, The Beatles and Dylan and high-level student activism had scarcely begun. Moreover, all through the 1960s, the term 'twentieth century' still seemed radically modern – even though the century was two-thirds over. Things were still conceived historically, on the premise of continuity. Because they had a sense of how things came to be, as well as being trained in sifting evidence, Honours History graduates were readily taken into External Affairs (as Foreign Affairs was quaintly termed, then) and the

Commonwealth public service. 'Only connect', EM Forster was frequently quoted as saying. But in fact everything *was* connected: we were merely the latest instalment. When I went into Ormond, a few senior students still occasionally wore old-fashioned felt hats. This sense of connectedness, even to the recent past, is now broken: as Howard Jacobson put it recently, we are a culture that has lost its sense of memory (as well as curiosity, and kindness). This was not so then, but things generally were so hidebound that something had to give.

India, empire, and its retreat was a big theme – enabling a flight from present entanglements and my personal evasions by offering instead a grand, bird's-eye view. This could be a fruitful kind of detachment: for my fourth-year thesis I had stumbled upon a conundrum. Why was it that, at the very beginning of the age of high imperialism, the British should voluntarily retreat from their occupation of a Boer republic? The topic also enabled me to explore South Africa – so the thesis did rather well, if subsequently better in London than it had in Melbourne. Gradually I was becoming aware of an irony: my father, through going to the ends of the earth, was (even if unwittingly) one of the last generation of Empire-builders; increasingly my interest was to try and work out what it had all meant. I was aware of a world out there – of Canada in particular, to some extent a variant of ourselves – which from a position of increased self-realisation was projecting a presence, as India already did. If the British Commonwealth really existed − beyond the litterati having accounts at Blackwell's in Oxford − then it had to be multipolar.

It wasn't the case, as I'd been taught at school, of India advancing towards self-government in ten (bestowed) steps; rather, the British had been squeezed out. I recalled the disconcerting picture repeatedly seen there in public places, of Subhas Chandra Bose, the leader of the Indian National Army, which had acted in collaboration with the Japanese. Indeed 'self-government' − even in quite elevated circles, well into the 1950s − was in fact a euphemism designed to minimise independence. When working on what would be a winning school essay for the Overseas League, I had fallen for this bullshit. I had doctored the conclusion my writing was leading to in order to conform to the prevailing Commonwealth ideology. But in 1965 I read Donald Horne, and was an instant republican.

At a certain level, Australia still merged into England. The BBC news was broadcast on the ABC, twice a day; I would listen, to get a broader perspective. There one would learn of 'constitutional talks' being held at Lancaster House, leading to the independence of Uganda… Botswana…the Gambia, and so on, down the line, each of these announcements sounding the tocsin of Empire. A friend of mine, with an anarchic sense of humour, proposed to write to Australian CBEs (Commanders of the

British Empire) simply asking, 'What have you done with it?' The same man toyed with the possibility of linking the revived Liberal Club at the University with the Liberal party in England, which he saw as being truer to traditional liberal values than the local conservatives. Such a blurring of identity seems extraordinary now, but there it was on my travel document: 'British Passport', in much bigger letters than the supplementary 'Australia'. I decided to put this to use when in Kathmandu, as a friend and I were in dire need of fuel for a short trekking expedition. The place had only six embassies, and an Australian one was not among them. So off we went to ask for assistance at the British Embassy. An official was a little surprised by the request, scratched his head, then complied — without charging us for the kerosene.

America held some curiosity for me — I regularly read the new, locally printed *New York Times Weekly Review*, novelists like Bellow, and responded to the measured prose as well as the argument of James Baldwin's essays. But a greater discovery was VS Naipaul, whose first book on India, *An Area of Darkness*, appeared some months after my return. Naipaul's intensity of response was accompanied by a strong sense of history, all set forth in Palladian prose.

Meanwhile England was entering our consciousness in quite new ways. Having given the world the word 'trendy', everyone was aware of Carnaby Street and The Beatles, while some of us followed the fortunes of the Wilson government. (If only there'd be a comparable Labor victory here!) But I did not see myself as an Anglophile. London's main interest to me was as the unchallenged classical music capital of the world.

It is worth recalling how undeveloped Australia was, high culturally, right to the end of the 1960s. There was no film industry; the Australian Film Development Corporation found it necessary to fund completely *The Adventures of Barry McKenzie* (which I saw most satisfactorily, filling in time on the Saturday of the Whitlam victory). A consistent stream of Australian plays had scarcely begun, while there would not have been twenty new novels published each year. If interested in the arts, you went to England for some kind of completion. It seemed you had to go − if only for a time. Sydney would not become a magnet − largely displacing London − till the 1970s, and the rise of American influence was still half a beat ahead.

In the meantime my life was on hold. I was concerned to gain acceptance in the History Department, where I was a tutor. Its academic centre of gravity, though weakening, was British History − of less interest to me than what was happening in the colonies and on the frontier. A great deal of the department's social life (though undoubtedly less than I realised) seemed to be spent by its members with each other. I was surprised to be categorised − dismissed − by one senior colleague as 'really a Sydney person'. But there were some who, with some justice, prided themselves on their sophistication. I heard that one of them had set a question on an exam paper which ran as follows: "'I love the Duke of Buckingham more than any other man" (James I). What were the political consequences of James's love for Buckingham?' A fair question, conceived as educative in the ways of the world. But somewhere along the line a committee seems to have downgraded love to 'high regard'. The tone of the department generally was very respectable. References to gays, at tea and elsewhere, could still be tacitly disapproving.

Such remarks could be matched by what gays said about themselves. I recoiled in horror from one man who, with characteristic self-loathing, spoke of a male couple living together as a 'bull camp' and a 'bitch camp'. Meanwhile my closest friend, after long periods of listlessness and a series of crises, had been consigned to shock treatment. Later I would learn of the novelist Janet Frame, who received some 200 ECT shocks in eight years. 'Each was equivalent in fear to an execution', she wrote. People told of a big piece of rubber being put in your mouth, and that afterwards you didn't wake up for twenty-four hours, then wandered around corridors wondering who you were. Shock treatment mangled memory, permanently; it was no way for an historian to go.

I was ripe for a fall. I became attached to a man two years younger, and whenever I returned to the college was always gladdened by the light streaming from his window.

Could this be – oh terrible beauty – love? In Ormond, such feeling had been diffused. Now it had an urgency – a pang – a sharp feeling in the chest (and elsewhere). It was a world I did not want to enter. I still had hopes, before moving overseas, of finding a girlfriend there. A new country would be a *tabula rasa*. This was not entirely baseless – years later I would meet an elderly Norwegian in France, and then met him again one day just over the border, in Italy. The Italian style and language released different elements in his personality, gave it a more powerful and more convincing projection; he should move the fifty ks, I joked. But some things lie too deep for such an easy resolution. As Virgil wrote, you can change your sky, but you can't change your nature.

'WE HAVEN'T GOT MUCH TIME', SAID THE ELFIN SIR KEITH Hancock, Australia's senior historian. 'Why do you wish to go to South Africa?' Are you a right-wing nutter?, he might have wondered. No, I was not. I did not say that I'd previously made inquiries at the new University of Malawi; nor anything about family connections, or general curiosity. Mine was the impeccable academic answer of working on the travel books of the historically-respected novelist Anthony Trollope, with a view to ascertaining how accurate they were as accounts of British settler societies – and how those societies were beginning to show signs of developing differently. 'Very well, I shall help you', Sir Keith replied, and did. Twelve months later I took up an acting-lectureship at Rhodes University at Grahamstown, in the Eastern Cape.

South Africa had always acted as a metonym for my sense of difference. Now it would become an adventure, as well as a kind of culmination. It was just after the assassination of the prime minister, Verwoerd, stabbed as he sat in parliament; talks between the British government and the settler regime in Rhodesia had just broken down. There was loose talk of sanctions perhaps enveloping the whole of southern Africa. My friend Neil Hyden gave me a facsimile copy of *Alice in Wonderland*: 'Brother Jim', he wrote, referring to the dedicatee, 'You will need to know about Wonderland where you are going'.

I realised that South Africa, with its two white ethnic groups, vast number of Africans, and Indians and Coloureds, would teach me much – not only about the British Empire, but also about complex societies and even, by inference, things about Australia. One of the reasons apartheid was able to work, I soon realised, was that the term 'South African' was never applied to anybody other than white people. To my horror, I realised the same semantic trick still operated in Australia – and was only beginning to be challenged, with the Aboriginal referendum held just after I left.

Contact across the colour line, particularly in a place

as small as Grahamstown, was difficult. You could not meet in cafes, pubs, or even sit on the same park bench. Somehow I made contact with an African clerk, who needed help with his correspondence course. So I arranged for him to come to my rooms – only to have the landlady express concern about what the neighbours might say, until I jollied her out of it. I'd hoped to get an insight into this man's life, but he firmly resisted all questioning – preferring instead to manipulate my liberal conscience.

I soon noticed, though, that there was a looser form of apartheid operating among white people. Segmentation existed everywhere. There were parallel English and Afrikaans organisations right through the society: in Cape Town, so few readers of the respective morning papers were presumed to read the other that they exchanged and published each other's editorials. The Afrikaners had the blacks under their thumb; but, still cultivating memories of the concentration camps of the Boer War, they were obsessed by the need to dominate the English-speakers. In fact they outnumbered them, but the English, so intricately wired to the wider world, were suspect in their loyalties.

And so I found myself witnessing the demise of the British Empire once again. One Afrikaner activist even spoke of ideally placing the English in an 'Anglostan', following the apartheid pattern of autonomous areas for blacks. Grahamstown was to be the centre of that, and it was building a huge memorial to its 1820 Settlers. A cult of 'Eighteen-twentology', as I came to call it, stressed their pioneering values, and implicitly downplayed their liberalism and their attachment to Britain. This was music to the government's ears: the hated Union Jack was never seen in this context, but rather the deconstructed flags of England, Scotland, and Ireland – the tribes of Britain, matching the (sub-)nations of Africa the Afrikaner Nationalists were striving to create. For the Afrikaners, running the country from their own organisations, the English South Africans were just white ballast. South Africa would never again have a non-Nationalist government, crowed BJ Vorster. Meanwhile the newspapers carried reports of one town council after another resolving that, since there had been no English-speaking member for so long, minutes of meetings would henceforth be released only in Afrikaans.

One day, on a return visit many years later, I was asked about my family over dinner. So I said what I knew, about my grandmother the Afrikaner. What was her maiden name? Woolf, I said. 'A *smous!*' (Jewish pedlar) exclaimed the sharpest of the group. The hostess got up from the table, and returned with an open Johannesburg phone book. She came over to me and ran her finger down a column of Woolfs. 'Jewish suburb', she said softly, 'Jewish suburb…Jewish suburb'. It was a shock. Jim had tried to embroider the name by adding a 'de' in front of it –

bringing it into line with that of some Melbourne people
he was trying to impress. But his more sophisticated sister,
Laura, had tumbled to what it was, and when I had asked
her said that her mother's maiden name was 'Dreyer' – an
Afrikaans name. I now recalled that an old family friend
had described my grandmother as 'German': perhaps she
was, though born in the South African Republic in 1885.
But Jewish? The names Frieda Francisca didn't suggest
this. But then another explanation came to mind. After a
half-hearted attempt at Jewish emancipation in Prussia –
rescinded with the demise of Napoleon – there were mass
conversions by Jews, mainly to ensure full civil rights.
Among them was Karl Marx's father; a Woolf ancestor
may have been another. Whatever the case, there remains
a puzzle: the only place where I have frequently seen
older men who look remarkably like my father has been
South Africa. Trimming his beard in his last years only
heightened the resemblance to elderly Afrikaners.

This revelation could have pole-axed my connection
with South Africa – except that the country had given
me so much. Shortly after arrival I was taken in hand by a
radical history lecturer, who cheerily dismissed any mis-
conceptions of mine as 'duck-billed platitudes'. Through
him I became good friends with an economist and then an
anthropologist – who provided a running commentary on
government policies and the evils of ideology. The dinner
table was a prime site of these educative conversations,

for there was no television (it might create a sense of envy among the blacks, said the Nationalists), and Grahamstown had only two cinemas. People had to create their own entertainment, and express their concerns about where the country was heading. Enlightened circles at Rhodes – by no means extending to the whole university – felt themselves encircled by the wider *laager* of Afrikaner wagons.

It was such a strange country: the radical lecturer, Graham Neame, used to say that it was everything from 1939 backwards. And it was tightly wired: Graham had a sister who came out of jail (as a member of the Communist Party) and went straight into exile – even as a more-distant relative of his was close to being the only English-speaking member of the Nationalist government. Things were always more complicated than one imagined. An Afrikaner woman, with a razor-thin racist mouth, was nevertheless capable within the space of two minutes of switching from Afrikaans to English to Xhosa, according to whom she was addressing. This was refreshing, after the then Australian presumption of sameness. But it was also so much less than it could have been: when I landed in Durban, I thought it might – given the multicultural ingredients – be a bit like Rio. Instead, the forces of repression made it more like a dowdier Brisbane.

Superficially, white Grahamstown with its late Georgian architecture could seem like Tasmania, with

jacarandas. (It contained a similar narrative of early importance and long decline.) But there was also the African
township, with its shanties sprawling ever further up and
over the opposite slope. It was one of the poorest in the
country; black children, dressed in sacks, would come and
beg in the High Street. Grahamstown was a place where
black Africa met Edwardian England; the old class system
was still in place, maintained by racial exploitation. And
as was the case a hundred years ago, there was real char-
itable effort by lots of (white) people; they sustained
over forty separate organisations. Moreover, respectable
middle-aged women became political activists. They
would don black sashes in memory of the violated con-
stitution, as they stood sternly with placards outside the
cathedral.

It was hard not to become fond of so quaint a place.
I soon dubbed the white ladies who regularly took tea
together (served by black maids) as the Gertie Circuit.
Grahamstown often yielded unexpected comedy. On
a return visit I was told of a young black man who was
delegated by the burglar-in-chief to keep an eye on the
elderly couple whose home they had invaded. Apparently he expressed admiration for the way the husband
was looking after his wife, confined to a wheelchair. They
became almost friendly. Then the woman asked, 'Young
man, do you go to church?' 'Yes', he replied, gun in hand.
'But I don't want to talk about that now.'

In writing this, I have come to see another reason why I took to Grahamstown. I have always been drawn to the phenomenon of different worlds touching, and this South African town brought together – as no other could – the elements of Olga's etiolated gentility and Jim's raw world of alien, oppositional cultures. There they were laid out side by side, in constant daily adjustment.

For all that, there was a deadly seriousness beneath the surface of everyday life. So brutally oppressive was apartheid that it normalised a degree of radicalism in me and others, sometimes unexpectedly. The local leaders of the national student union would in Australia have passed for Liberals; but the logic of their position compelled them to enunciate basic liberal principles which were anathema to the (white) government: they got better and better at it. Three of them, whom I often shared a meal with, were deported or had their passports taken away. But it was worse than that. The Afrikaner rector of nearby Fort Hare, the oldest black university in the country, in 1968 suspended hundreds of students; a solidarity march from Grahamstown was organised. But at the last minute a public meeting was called. It was addressed by Donald Woods, editor of the most radical newspaper in the country. The government had brought in raw recruits to the local army camp, he said, back-country Afrikaners who have no love for the English South Africans. If you were to march, there is no guarantee that, on a lonely country road, they wouldn't comply with an order to fire on you. Sadly, he added, I recommend that you call off the march. Reluctantly, the meeting did so. Nine years later Woods himself felt compelled to flee the country.

The time came for me to return to Melbourne, much more confident. At one stage I had not seen another Australian for nine months, and so had created a new context for myself. I was well aware of my sexuality, now, but had done nothing to advance it. South Africa was difficult enough, with the Special Branch actively fishing for information, without seeking to complicate one's life further. I did become passionately attached to a young man, who subsequently has always remained a firm friend; we see each other now when he comes to visit a daughter in Sydney. There was enough idealism in that relationship for it to survive physical disappointment. An Ideal Friend – that's what I was after – one with whom one would cross the boundary into sexuality. Others have had this fantasy, including the he-man writer Jack London, who dreamed of a companion with whom he might share physical adventure, emotional intensity, and perhaps…Swept away by Gluck's musical expression of the friendship of Orestes and Pylades, I'd absorbed the classical Greek version of this without quite realising it. But all this was too rarefied, and a deep device (I now realise) to outpace, or reverse, internalised shame. It was a galaxy away from everyday life. On Australian television appeared a medical thug called Lovibond, who in a flat voice intoned the merits of curing homosexuality by electric shock treatment. My own remedy – at last – was enactment, just before leaving for England and in South Africa on the way.

I DIDN'T HAVE RESULTS GOOD ENOUGH TO GET ME TO Oxford or Cambridge – and, apart from the academic prestige, didn't have any strong inclination to go there. For all their excellencies, they might turn out to be, in some ways, greater Grahamstowns. (The Rhodes history department was run like a prep school for Oxford.) I didn't want to become Englished; but I did want to live in the big world-city, London. Going there was less a culmination than simply moving to the other end of the spectrum. It was not, as Peter Conrad described his crossing of Waterloo Bridge, 'the exact moment of my birth'. I had been inoculated against Anglophilia by having taken the long way round, via India and South Africa.

February 1970 was an odd time to arrive in London. 'Swinging London' had slackened, so much so that Edward Heath and the Conservatives surprised everybody by winning a thumping majority at the polls in June. Before his term ended, Heath would take on the miners: the subsequent power shortages resulted in a three-day working week. It was winter. People would move around London's darkened streets – past terraces that looked as if they were destined to crumble into the Thames – as if in a smudgy nineteenth-century lithograph. Britain's problems seemed overwhelmingly economic. The great hope was that entry into the Common Market (the European Union) might guarantee a brighter future. Otherwise there was the alarming portent of Liverpool, where the decline of the colonial trade and the impact of technology were bringing about the collapse of the port.

In England the old order had a critical mass far greater than in the broader Commonwealth: the cultural consequences of the loss of Empire would come more slowly. They could shock when they did. I remember going to visit a once-famous musical library attached to an Anglican theological college, to find the library long gone and the carpets rolled up. More strikingly, the buildings were up for sale.

It gradually dawned on me – as I mulled upon the title of a recent novel of Nadine Gordimer's, *The Late Bourgeois World* – that the one I was moving in was the Late British World. This was brought home sharply by seeing Fellini's *Satyricon*, not long after my arrival. I was struck by the variety of languages heard fleetingly in the film – unusual, then – and strongly felt that there was an implicit analogy between the Roman world depicted there and the multicultural one that was about to burst upon us. Meanwhile, a friend mentioned how, doing the rounds of the secondhand bookshops, he had been able to pick up a book which had belonged to Lord Cromer, the British proconsul in Egypt; another told of a wistful book on an Indian hill station that had belonged to EM Forster. Imperial associations lay in clumps – and dumps – all around me.

But it was the present context, rather than the high noon of Empire, that became my imaginative world. I began to think that, as far as Australia was concerned, we ought to have a better, subtler word than decolonisation, since that was largely a matter of the restoration of full political authority to a once-subject people. Given that we had been settled from the British Isles and numbered among the British dominions, I thought the term for us should be 'de-dominionisation'. A clumsy word (blame the Brits), but a useful one for identifying the process of a natural growth towards independence, within a context of declining affinities and divergent interests.

Working at the Institute of Commonwealth Studies, and writing a broader thesis on Trollope, I soon became aware of that divergence of interests, or at least perspective. For a place mostly concerned with policy, in its current and historical dimensions, they were good to me: but my supervisor gave no encouragement to talk of de-dominionisation, and right then that was what I really wanted to get off my chest. (Discussion with Canadians in particular had convinced me of its contemporary reality.) In the end, the perspectives of the place were British – and events in Australia were quickening with the lead-up to the Whitlam election of 1972. I was in the wrong place and in the wrong discipline.

My vantage point for some of this period was London House, a vast residence for Commonwealth and American male postgraduate students and academics on sabbatical leave. It had been established by a trust set up by a chairman of Barclays Bank. Designed by Herbert Baker (Cecil Rhodes' favourite architect) it managed to be both grand and hum-drum at the same time, except for a dining hall which – complete with Empire crests and a portrait of Jan Smuts – was genuinely lofty and magnificent despite its fustian decoration. It was now the grandest of cafeterias, the animated conversation of men (and women) in their early to mid-twenties paying scant regard to the imperial rhetoric high above their heads. There a group of us would gather each morning to read the excellent reports in *The Times*, following the progress (if that was the word) of the 1971 Springbok rugby tour of Australia. It couldn't go on, we all agreed (even some conservatives). And so we formed a mock coalition government in exile – to make the point before residents from other countries (most headed for elite jobs on return) that many Australians did not approve of what the Liberal and Country party governments were doing. Some of them had seen a major article on Australia in *Time* magazine, which in passing referred to an interview with Prime Minister Billy

McMahon. The writer had asked for his ideas on the future of Australia. McMahon, mumbling, got up and went over to his filing cabinet, and looked under 'F' for Future. He found nothing.

Some wit had described London House as 'the biggest gay hotel in London', but in the earliest 1970s there was little evidence of it. That would change, but gay militancy took a little while to cross the Atlantic after the Stonewall riots of 1969. My first recognition of it was seeing a ginger-bearded young man, in high boots, floral dress and a handbag, standing near the edge of the platform in the Tube. (No-one seemed to bat an eyelid.) My own coming out was slow: it was some time before I plucked up the courage to enter a gay pub. At the same time, I had not given up hope that I would have a 'normal' relationship. In the free-floating world of London, it became possible to have affairs with two women; later I had a great female friend. But my basic impulse, I had to recognise, drove me towards men. I soon realised that, in the world as it was then constituted, this would mean I wouldn't have children. Shedding that option turned out to be much easier than I would have thought.

But other things were difficult. There were many things I had to *un*learn: the prime one being that erotic relationships were less complicated than the friendships I had often opted for. I learned that in sexual matters a pass is usually called a pass when it fails. Meanwhile I came to realise that being bashful was no good: so I broke up the word, re-arranged it, to become full of bash. As a member of the Gay Liberation Front (GLF) I went once or twice with a partner to straight dances, to drive a wedge into existing public spaces. The reception was not always cordial, but surprisingly other people would always spring to our defence. The counter-culture was not just a generational matter in England, as it tended to be in Australia; often it fingered long-standing grievances.

As it happened, the Camden Town GLF met the same night as a particularly good gay disco. So I'd say to my friend Jamie – who had a car – which shall it be? Camden or Camberwell? Madcap or Redcap? Then off we'd go...I had one-night stands, and affairs – notably with a nephew of EM Forster (he was, as it were, 'in the family way'). But a more usual problem was bound up in the English class system. I found working-class men the warmest, but didn't have much in common with them; on the other hand, middle-class people I found rather bloodless, brittle, and if interested in cultural matters, voracious trendies. Since I had already dubbed England Pom de terre, it was not surprising that I should come across Pom deterrents.

A number of times through these years I went to performances of *Carmen*. And – whether at the Coliseum, Covent Garden, or in Cape Town or Milan, there I would hear it – the harp, accompanying the duet, 'Speak to me of my mother'. It would always break me up: it's the only moment in the opera when the harp has any prominence. As much as Micaela was for Don Jose, it was a marker of how far I had travelled in every sense, and came like a gentle reproach.

Apart from opera and classical music, London offered so much. You could stumble upon something fresh and appealing, and follow it through to undreamed-of heights. Thus it was for me with Chekhov plays: after seeing *Uncle Vanya*, since an Australian friend had a major part in it, I was able to see another half dozen in less than a year. But I cannot say that I really *liked* the place, except for a few corners here and there. Myddelton Square was one of them: there I lived in a large room in a Georgian terrace (£3 a week), overlooking a decorous church, its clock-tower becoming my great-grandfather clock. But I could get no conversation out of other people met on the stair-case, even after being there a year. I suspect I became a bit of a Steppenwolf figure, to cite Hermann Hesse's cult novel of the time, for I read it with flashes of recognition.

Although shortly after I arrived a man on the phone chivvied me for describing myself 'a foreigner', I knew within a week or two I wouldn't stay. (It wasn't just the dirty cotton-wool skies.) When in 1971 Judge Argyle jailed the editors in the *Oz* obscenity trial, I was livid when a group of expatriates – headed by Clive James – wrote a letter to *The Times*, opposing it and saying (their supposed clincher) that this kind of judgement was precisely the reason why the undersigned had left Australia. The Poms had done it all by themselves, but somehow this lot turned the case into another stick to beat Australia with. It was more infuriating than another incident two years later, when there was a student demonstration against the Minister for Education – 'Margaret Thatcher, milk snatcher!' The Australian Union of Students had an active international presence in those days, and sent a telegram of support. When the solidarity messages were duly read out, it was a case of 'Oh, there's one here from Australia!' The audience received it with hoots of laughter.

FROM LONDON I DUTIFULLY KEPT UP A CORRESPONDENCE with both parents. At this time people used aerogrammes: cheaper blue forms with an imprinted stamp, on flimsy air-mail paper. Folded, they were roughly postcard size. One day an Indian friend spied a number of Australians reading their letters, and noticed a new, wider format. 'Perfect!' he declared. 'The right size for mothers…England keeps to the right size, for sons.' Olga's letters were sprightly, often like humorous asides, dashed off fragments of conver-sation. Once, I addressed a letter to her in Whorethorn, knowing that the postcode would ensure delivery. It did. On her next she said nothing but wrote out the address in full, delicately placing an eyelash under the 'Haw' of the suburb's name. She was lonely, after Tasma's sudden death and Norma's serious stroke. But she took an interest in what was happening, approving of the Vietnam moratorium and declaring that – for the first time in her life – she would be voting Labor.

Jim's letters were also affectionate. He even said how important I had been as a stabilising force when he had lived alone at Monash Avenue. But the predominant note was always the possibility of disaster – the poorly handled economy (by government, but particularly by Labor), the unions, his liquidity problems, and the periodic serious illnesses he had always sustained. He wrote of my job prospects, occasionally enclosing advertisements for positions. His joy, apart from going north, lay in his two young sons.

It was on their account that he wrote to tell me, a few months after I had left for London, that he had drawn up a new will. In it he would leave me just $1000; I had had my education, whereas the boys were still to have theirs. But if he were still around by the time they got through university (unlikely), then on the death of his wife the estate would be split three ways. 'Felt you should know this', he concluded. Well, yes; most fathers would have discussed the matter with their son before he left. There wasn't much I could do (intended); and so I acquiesced. At the heart of the change lay a certain rough justice. But a subsequent letter spoke of the fear of my predeceasing the boys, and the money going to 'some outsider'. (Always

the external threat.) And from there it was a simple pro-
gression to cutting me out of the will altogether – by
giving me the $1000 now, while I was in London, since it
might then be of greater use. I was in no position to argue,
being so far away – and had suspected that the needs of
the second family would always take priority. A clairvoy-
ant once told me – in a surprised tone – that when she
saw my generation, she got the numbers one, and three.
Truly it was so. I could never count on Jim seeing it as a
simple three.

When I returned briefly at the end of 1972 – partly
drawn by the Whitlam election, plus the need to make
inquiries about jobs – I decided I would also tell my father
about my sexuality. I would sugar the pill by saying that
I was bisexual; there was just enough truth in that for it
not to replace one deception with another. Somehow the
opportunity came in the course of a chat in the kitchen.
He said that he had imagined that one day – possibly
quite early given the disruption with Olga – I would come
and tell him I was marrying, as I wanted to start a family
of my own. But he seemed to take it calmly, saying he
had always half-suspected it. He asked when had I first
felt the attraction towards men; while the conversation
soon veered off to other matters, he referred back to this
declaration a couple of times in a frank and sympathetic
fashion, showing that he had assimilated it.

It did not occur to me that this would be another

instance of the absorptive part of the vindictive style. I returned to England almost immediately. I didn't hear from him for quite a while. What did turn up was a letter from a psychiatrist, informing me that my father had told him about my problem (him?), and that I should come and see him when I'd returned. I was pretty annoyed, and threw it away. It was the tip of an iceberg.

III

Pieces of silver

And a man's foes shall be they of his own household.

Matthew 10:36

*If you succeed in cheating someone, don't think them a fool…
realise that person trusted you more than you deserved.*

Hobart sandwich board, 2016

VISITORS DIDN'T NOTICE THE MUSKET AT FIRST. BUT IT was there – with an invented provenance originating in the Zulu War – just above the front door, positioned as if to defend hearth and home. The next thing for any frontiersman to do was to extend the perimeters, and this my father did. The house overlooked a golf course, and beyond that spread a valley: a street theoretically ran along the boundary. Immediately in front lay one of the holes; occasionally the odd golf ball would lob in the vegetable garden. This was regarded as a bombardment, or at least a threat, so the golf club was compelled to relocate the green. That done, it now became possible to encroach upon the right of way: Father fenced some of it in, looking to claim it by adverse possession. (Other neighbours tentatively followed suit, till the land came to be legally transferred by the council.)

Visitors passed through the front door to a large L-shaped room, which gradually became a study in brown. Offset by the turquoise blue of the carpet, there were brown walls, brown bark paintings, and even a brown Dadda – he liked a brown jacket (and suit), with brownish ties or tan shirts. The colours might have suited him as a young man, when there was a touch of ginger in his moustache; but now with his grey hair (where there was some) they seemed incongruous, a bit too emphatic. It didn't matter – such colours proclaimed his imaginative universe.

Against the near wall was an antiquated radiogram, rarely played. When it finally packed up it was not replaced, but functioned as a stand from time to time for artworks. The visitor, moving forward into the room, would have his attention drawn to the far wall, past the smart Danish chairs and the Trobriand Islands table, to the bookshelves ranged above the combustion stove, with their erratic collection. Beyond, the view outside was given little access by the notably small windows: the house was built straight after the war, when glass was scarce. And so they were replaced with double doors, a pergola being added outside. My father soon decided to enclose part of that, confiscating the view. He created for himself a splendid study, where he would surround himself with bark paintings, didjeridus, clubs, woomeras, boomerangs and other Aboriginal implements. And so he would sometimes be photographed, ready to hold court.

IN 1961, SOUTH AFRICA BECAME A REPUBLIC. JIM HAD NOT held a passport for years, and thought he had better determine his citizenship. He was assured that, while born there, it had been as a British subject, and so his status remained unchanged. In fact South Africa had always lingered in his consciousness: one of the few political figures that he spoke of approvingly was the recent South African prime minister Jan Christian Smuts. He was a world figure, much more so than Robert Menzies, and as a former Boer general who had come to believe in the Empire, was more completely taken to the bosom of the British establishment. His voice was familiar, too, from popular wartime broadcasts. My father noted the old man's astonishing political defeat, his death soon after, and bought and read the biography his son wrote immediately afterwards. As a counterpoint there was another book called *Jungle Man*, by PJ Pretorius, full of hunting adventures. Southern Africa had not died for Jim.

Moreover, it had in recent years been the site for the last great venture in imperial architecture. The Central African Federation, inaugurated in 1953, linked the (white) self-governing colony of Southern Rhodesia to the essentially black (but firmly white-ruled) territories of Northern Rhodesia and Nyasaland. There was much talk of 'racial partnership'. But Jim ignored the rhetoric – as white Rhodesians themselves were disposed to do – sensing it would be business as usual. He must have picked up on the fact that, with South Africa now ruled by the Afrikaner Nationalists, Southern Rhodesia was 'going ahead'. White migrants were pouring in – had begun to do so as refugees from Britain's postwar Labour government – so markedly that even as late as 1970 some seventy-five per cent of Rhodesian whites over the age of sixteen had been born elsewhere. It was commonly said that it took only half an hour for a migrant to become a Rhodesian.

It was all about lifestyle – the sunshine, swimming pools and servants.

Jim had never lost touch with a branch of the family living in Southern Rhodesia (Zimbabwe), and now this intensified. In addition to the Christmas cards came annual illustrated magazines, brochures and the occasional calendar. In the Monash Avenue years, with his marriage stalemated and his job at the Forests Commission giving him little satisfaction, he would fantasise about migrating there. He told me about the servants – I would never have to do the lawn again! – and then produced a booklet on Umtali (Mutare) where the cousins lived. With its emphasis on amenity and modernity, to me it looked like a rather 'progressive' Australian town. Where were the black people?, I asked. They lived in their own section of town, I was told. That was a puzzle to me. To Jim it was simply a well-ordered society.

By the time I left school, with the live-in ladies and then his second marriage, Jim's Rhodesian fixation had lessened. But it remained at the back of his mind, if only as a romantic option. Films such as *Walk Into Paradise* (starring Chips Rafferty) and *His Majesty O'Keefe* (Burt Lancaster) kept the fantasy alive. Later, he was annoyed with me for having gone to South Africa and not gone the extra mile, so to speak, to see the cousins in Rhodesia. But they were ardent supporters of white supremacist Ian Smith, and had sent us aerogrammes plastered with propaganda;

it seemed a long way to go for an argument. When contact between the two branches of the family subsequently fell away, I was not forgiven.

SOUTH AFRICA, RHODESIA, AUSTRALIA, FIJI, NEW GUINEA... Jim's world was the (British) southern hemisphere, the word British placed in brackets because England itself was conspicuously absent from it. He admired Churchill, and could – with light satire – imitate the Upper English manner. But he never had the slightest desire to go there. He found things to like in Italy, and was drawn to a certain French style (its declaratory nature would have suited his personality). But he never went to continental Europe either. It was not that he identified strongly with this country. Indeed, he never described himself as 'an Australian'. No, for much of his life Jim thought of himself first and foremost as a white man; the lands he knew were 'the white man's world'.

Built into this was the idea of a 'white man's country', which was a dynamic one. In South Africa it had already been achieved, gradually drawing the two hostile white groups closer and closer together to defend it; in Kenya the phrase was heard as colonists staked out their claim to what became known as the White Highlands. *Making* a place a white man's country – in effect fit for wives and children – was what it was about. For this, in addition to physical toughness, the frontiersman needed an element of ruthlessness combined with occasional recklessness: you had to dominate, assert the primacy of the white man, show you would stop at nothing to achieve it. The boast was that 'I know the native' – privileged, hard-won information (much of it appropriated), and knew how to manipulate him. 'Natives', after all, were pre-rational in their thought, 'primitive' people, the embodiment of 'the childhood of Man'.

The more I read about 'the white man' the more I recognised my father. Like so many boys across the Empire – right up to the 1950s, when Biggles was still taking flight – he grew up on imperial romances. Rider Haggard's Umslopogaas, the worthy black adversary, was kept alive on that Tasmanian orchard – a memory, as he became, of South Africa. But other legendary figures were also shaped to purpose. When a small boy I was told of Ulysses, the archetypal wanderer; apart from a hint that he nearly went to water over Circe, it was his battle with the Cyclops that Jim kept returning to, fixated on the hero's resourcefulness as the pole was thrust into the giant's one great eye. Life on the frontier had also endorsed Jim's constant self-dramatisation, his sense of himself as the centre of the action. Just thinking about things, he believed, never got you anywhere – unless it was with strategic purpose. So he despised Arts graduates as ineffectual ditherers. Meanwhile a classic pith helmet (a topee) lay about the house – something he rarely wore, now, since he knew it had become an object of ridicule. But he could not bear to part with it.

What propelled Jim towards the frontier? Partly it was the sense of adventure, felt particularly keenly by macho types who drifted towards 'the Islands', as New Guinea and Fiji in particular were called in Australia at the time. Among them was the young Errol Flynn, for there was an unusually high proportion of ratbags – balanced by some idealists, who went as missionaries. (A generation or more later, both elements were still evident in frontier universities.) In Jim's case, there was the additional fact that he tended to be an individualist, a non-joiner, a non-believer: the attachments to his own culture were not strong. There were also more personal elements. The death of his mother had come as a shock: apart from his attachment to her, she was the authority figure in the family. Shattered, after a breakdown he emerged even more hardened, and with a need to replace that lost authority – preferably by exercising it himself. In later life it was apparent in the way he wrote, carefully, in spurts – every stroke of the pen heavy with import, as if signing away half a kingdom.

The question arises, of his younger days, did Jim have sex across the colour line? The answer may very well have been no, at least not on a regular basis. I suspect that the main reason he romanticised Daru – a small island administrative post near the mouth of the Fly River – was that there (once he came down periodically from uncontrolled territory) he would have had a fling, but probably with white women. It was part of the mystique that interracial sex could be regarded as taboo. Besides, for a white man on the move it complicated things, created obligations, slowed you down.

Women tended to be regarded as accessories. Tellingly, when white women first turned up in India in large numbers, they just received an add-on to the title 'sahib' – applied to white men – and became madam, or 'mem sahibs'. There was also a sense that women repressed man's vital nature; the Samson and Delilah story, which everybody then would have known, pointed to darker deceits. So even when they were loved, they were often resented.

Jim in those years – his late twenties – seems to have responded to their absence in two ways. Olga, his distant beloved, became a fixation; he set her in concrete. Nearer at hand was the boy Uau (Wow), who seems to have attached himself to him. Quite often willing young helpers presented themselves to explorers and frontiersmen – enterprising kids who were shallowly rooted in their families, and wanted to identify with the white man's rising power and authority. HM Stanley (he who found Livingstone) became so attached to his *protégé* that he wrote a book about him. Sometimes there would have been sex, but more strikingly a close emotional bond

would develop between the man and the aspiring, compliant boy. It was intense, but unthreatening. Jim commonly spoke of Uau all through my childhood, fondly.
In 1954, when we were walking cross-country in New
Guinea, a curious seven-year-old followed us at a discreet
remove. Just like Uau, said my father. You could train him
to do anything for you.

Had Jim experienced the tug of temptation? Unlikely,
but he would have recognised its reality. He was embar-
rassed by any public acknowledgement on my own part of
homosexuality. Jim's hostility towards it was real, and arose
from a sense of its being the ultimate subversion. Homosexuality was the greatest confuser of categories, whereas
the frontiersman always saw things with the fiercest clar-
ity. It offended his sense of uncompromising masculinity,
the manliness essential to maintaining whiteness. For Jim
was just as dismissive of 'coloured' people; that is to say,
people of mixed ancestry. Hybridity was suspect. In Lae, a
part-indigenous, part-Chinese storekeeper, eyeing us with
curiosity as he set about his work, thereby confirmed – in
Jim's view – his innate untrustworthiness.

In addition to the camaraderie of white associates –
conscious that they formed a butch aristocracy – a frontiersman could feel a real attraction towards the people
being brought under control. Jim always spoke of indigenous people who were 'unspoilt' – unpolluted by white
contact. For him, the values of traditional societies

were enduring – they were timeless, eternal. He had an utterly static view of them – a view some anthropologists, particularly in South Africa, also advanced. Once he found Arnhem Land, it became an adventure playground, his dreamtime. There existed a world of firm male authority, where kinship was of prime importance in determining social role, and where a sense of community was centred on participatory rituals with their attendant mysteries. It was a world of hard, 'primitive' values – realising, in its own way, a right-wing fantasy. Aborigines were to be envied.

As he went back year after year (escaping the Melbourne winter) Jim gained greater and greater acceptance. It was the Yolngu practice to selectively reveal aspects of their culture to chosen whites. Jim's boast was that he became 'initiated' into a tribe, although in print he tempered this to being 'accepted' into a named clan and moiety. 'I will never forget', he wrote, 'the thrill of encountering the whispered "inside" language used to discuss sacred matters'. Earlier he used to say – dubiously – that he was a Freemason. This was much better. And while he may not have been 'initiated', he did develop real and deep friendships among the Yolngu. Just as white and black South Africans in the apartheid era were inevitably drawn to each other at London parties, so Jim found his other. He craved for, and found, completion. Arnhem Land was a place where he felt comfortable and balanced, both privileged and accepted. There, at last, he sat down with Umslopogaas.

JIM WAS TOUGH. IN FACT HE WAS A BATTERED MAN. HE survived for sixty years on one kidney; had broken his leg and pelvis in 1934, said he had broken his leg three times. Years after it was found that in the last accident he had broken both legs; one had gone undetected. Soundings, to clear his urethra from recurring impediments, were once performed in front of me (a lesson in the stern realities of life), as he lay on the floor probing his cock with a formidable-looking metal object. There were many other diseases, long spells in hospital every so often, together with the constant discipline imposed by diabetes for his last twenty years. His response was to emphasise the imperative of action. The life force was strong within him.

What is striking about Jim is the way that, in stout middle age, he set about refashioning himself completely. He had done a similar thing at the age of nineteen, after the nervous breakdown following the death of his mother. But this one was more thorough-going. His 'discovery' of Arnhem Land was only one of the things of importance that happened to him in the four years up to 1962. (This was despite contracting encephalitis.) He divorced, remarried, had children (and was delighted to correct those who mistook him for their grandfather), and also shed his hated daytime job as a draftsman in the Forests Commission. In the few years when he was just past fifty, he acquired a new home, a new life, a new wife.

IT IS NOT CLEAR WHERE JIM MET EVE, BUT IT WAS PROBABLY in connection with adult education classes. A great enthusiast, he would talk about New Guinea (refreshed for him by the coffee boom), and in Melbourne ran a Travel Group (talks and slides). Eve may have gone along to that. A commercial artist, she worked at a studio in town. A believer in self-improvement, she would save up to buy (as many people then did) the new long-playing records of classical music. Her closest friend was a biologist, a woman who – most unusually then – had gone on an early foreign aid scheme to work in Indonesia. They probably shared political views, amongst other things; Eve thought of herself as a democratic socialist.

Jess was still living with him when Jim began seeing Eve: he soon gave Jess her marching orders. After his flirtation with the squattocracy, someone of more solid stock had particular appeal. Eve's father was a bluff builder, genial but careless about the house, which was perpetually 'unfinished'; her mother was an anxious-looking woman. Eve inherited her small stature; was bustling and purposeful, and dressed practically in slacks. Over a strong jaw she had appealing brown eyes, and a pleasant, subtle smile; she was less anxious than appraising. Generally she spoke in short sentences, occasionally breaking into what was less of a laugh than a cackle. Although her own art was pleasant and descriptive, she was drawn to the faces of Modigliani. Those slit eyes and blank faces looked pretty much alike to me, their severity a form of distancing from the world.

Although she spent the weekends with Jim, Eve always went home. She was holding him off. Marriage was what she wanted – she was now in her early thirties, still living with her parents, and wanted to avoid being left on the shelf. This was her last opportunity. The fact that Jim lopped years off his age (as Olga had done) added to the attractiveness of the match. Eve fell under Jim's spell: 'I would have crossed rivers and climbed mountains for him', she said later.

For his part, Jim was determined that this time he would get it right. 'Behind every successful man stands a good woman', he'd say, knowing he had found one. He would put paid to the old fear, the haunting vision of the empty house. There would be children. He wanted to start a dynasty – tellingly, the first name at the head of the tree in the family Bible was James Davidson. Only recently I realised that as a child he must have pored over it many times, and absorbed it. For the birth date given there (in Melbourne, 1845) is 31 March – one which (requiring only slight adjustment) he would make his own birthday.

The Afrikaners have a word for it – *stamvader* – founder of the line. So Jim saw himself.

Jim was so eager to get cracking that once, in the lounge, he began fondling Eve and talking about having children. It was as if I wasn't there. Shocked, I reacted strongly. Eve left the room. It was only a month or two after my parents' divorce and my father's remarriage: the pace of it all was just a little too quick for me, still a schoolboy. All Jim could see was that I had upset Eve. I was being 'selfish', should consider other people...And must apologise. (I did.) Not for the first time I had to assume the adult role, simply saying I needed time to get used to things. He said nothing to that, but seethed.

There was no problem with Eve. We got on well: talked and laughed together. Once, shortly after they were married, we went off on a long Sunday afternoon walk. When we arrived back at the house, Jim was out the front. 'I don't think he likes us walking together', she said, under her breath. It didn't happen again. I was surprised by the necessity of the aside. She was his; all our relatives were his. (In fact, even my mother's were his, when it suited.)

Eve fell in with this. When once I brought up the subject of his previous women, she firmly put her foot down. She didn't want to know. This was a partnership, a compact, and everything previous was irrelevant. She never spoke of her own family, unless asked. They rarely visited: her brother would come over occasionally, but suddenly

he died, shortly after being badly electrocuted. The compact would be ratified by two miniature silhouettes, one
of each of them, placed adjacent to the marital bed. Olga
had never received this treatment. But Eve was younger,
tougher, and brought the promise of children. She loved
her 'Bukzi'. They had a good, if business-like sex life: func-
tional sounds would emanate from the bedroom, should
the door be casually left open.

FOR THEIR DELAYED HONEYMOON, IN 1960, THEY WENT TO
Central Australia. Alice Springs was then the prime des-
tination of the tourist trade; the film *A Town Like Alice* had
caught the mood. Jim ventured beyond, to Ayers Rock
(Uluru), not much visited then. There he had met and
chatted with the writer Bill Harney, capturing the conversation on tape; two old hands talking to each other. Then
at Hermannsburg he met, amongst others, sons of Albert
Namatjira, Ewald and Enos, painters themselves. Instinctively Jim had a good eye – all those years at the theodo-
lite, and as a draftsman and mapmaker. But his tastes in art
were unfocused. Now Eve, a professional, was at his side;
it gave him the confidence to embark on a new venture.
Together they bought some of these Namatjira watercolours, and took them back to Melbourne.

After being fairly indifferent to them, Jim had gradually become more curious about the Aborigines.

Somewhere he met Pastor Doug Nicholls, and became involved for a time in the Aboriginal Advancement League. He was active in helping to build a girls' hostel in Westgarth. But he was not happy with the people he had to work with – a feeling probably quite reciprocal – and used a recent illness as an excuse to resign. Around this time, he had begun to slip into anecdotage – Queenstown, Thursday Island, Fiji, Daru...His new passion for Aboriginal art provided a much-needed focus. For one thing, it provided a clear basis for respecting black people.

Shortly after returning to Melbourne, Jim called on Ruth McNicoll at the Argus Gallery. 'Could you put on a show for me?' he inquired, explaining that he had dozens of paintings by the Arunta (Arrernte), the people of Namatjira. McNicoll was cagey; bring in a few, she said. In he came with a number, which he proceeded to arrange around the floor. 'No, Mr Davidson', she said, 'I couldn't sell them and I really don't much like them. But if you can get the real thing that Aborigines traditionally do – barks – then I would be interested'. Aware of the convergence between his new wife's work and Aboriginal watercolours, Jim stiffened: 'No-one would be interested in those!' he declared. But before long he came back with some. They sold like hot cakes. An Art Gallery of New South Wales exhibition of barks had just been touring the country; shortly after he would put on one of his own at the Argus Gallery.

By 1962 Jim had made his first journey to Arnhem Land, and thereafter bark paintings were the core of his business – and interest. The barks fitted in well with the Islander weapons and objects that were already a feature of the big L-shaped room. And they enabled Jim to connect with 'primitive' people once more; nearly always he went north alone. Domestically, this new twist to the handling of Aboriginal art reasserted his primacy. Eve meanwhile painted a huge mural in the Coolibah Room at the Southern Cross Hotel, drawing on bark paintings. The appropriation involved in this was matched by her own relegation: the time would come when he would not allow her to thread her way past the didjeridus into his study. Even so, the balance of the marriage, and children, combined with the annual walkabout to Arnhem Land, finally steadied Jim. There was no more talk of moving away from Melbourne. He had found a design for living that suited him. He turned his house into a gallery, the first in Melbourne devoted primarily to Aboriginal art. Friends were now unequivocally replaced by 'contacts'. The trickle of customers, which included surprises like the famous pianist Claudio Arrau, stroked his ego.

At the same time, he became something of an authority. He might rise to his feet to make a statement at some academic occasion, but as he spoke an involuntary jingling of the coins in his pocket revealed his uncertainty.

Jim had always craved recognition as an original, and as some kind of guru. To this was now added a sense of imparting (or withholding) mysteries. The claim to initiation was his qualification, the barks he brought back from Arnhem Land his own version of Bring 'Em Back Alive. For a man almost devoid of a spiritual dimension, the mystery that was present in these paintings, their apparent sophistication extending far beyond their primitive forms, were what transfixed him. He had no interest in what art critics might have to say: even a two-volume work on primitivism in twentieth-century art that I gave him sparked little interest. He could supply the essential cultural dimension himself.

When I had been in South Africa, an anthropologist friend of mine pointed to the writings of Saxe Bannister, and said I should take note: land rights were the great sleeper in Australia. But apart from the fact that my interests lay elsewhere, there was the fact that Father – rather like the Führer with Bohemia and Moravia – had already proclaimed a protectorate over the Aborigines. I didn't dare go near them: too often he and I would look at the same set of facts, and draw precisely the opposite conclusions. Besides, he patrolled the frontiers of that territory quite rigorously. Later, when he told me he had written an article for the *Art Bulletin of Victoria*, I congratulated him. I said I'd like to see it.

'You can buy one at the Gallery.'

'I haven't got time to go to the Gallery.'

'I feel insulted.' (Soft chortle – half-joking, don'tcha know!)

'In that case you insult easily.'

So Arnhem Land was his. I was never told much about it. Mawalan and Mathaman (brothers), with Narritjin, were bark painters who became close friends and household words; there were others, but these names were uttered almost as an invocation in themselves. I now know he won their confidence, listened to them carefully, sometimes sat beside them as they painted; drove them about in his ute, was taken to their country, living off fish, pigeon, crabs, crays. He loved every minute of it – it was country 'still barred to white men', he excitedly wrote to me (in London). Publicly, my father saluted Mathaman as 'a man of the greatest integrity, who would die for you if he liked you, but would kill you, if he did not'.

For Jim, Narritjin had the same *mana*, since he had been a member of the group who years before had killed a party of Japanese pearlfishers. He was also a fine artist; beyond that, the 'keeper' of the clan designs. Jim told how Narritjin heroically took a letter to Darwin officialdom – 'living off the land and swimming crocodile and shark-infested waters'. The heroic mission was an attempt to stave off bauxite mining. But it was doomed. Around this time, standing on top of a rock scrutinising the new landscape with another friend, Munggurrawuy, Jim could see 'the distress on his face, and realised I was witnessing the final destruction of an ancient, mystical, non-materialistic culture that was probably the oldest in the world...'. There was a touch of Victorian pathos about this ('The Last of His Tribe'), but it heightened Jim's own sense of mission, of making the culture known.

Jim would argue with me that Australians had to become like the Aborigines. Rather than being a high-flown Jindyworobak approach, he meant it almost literally. In my father's view, the whole nation should be sharing in Aboriginal rituals and pastimes, as he had done. It never would, of course (although it would later make a number of gestures in that direction). In the meantime his own position became more central – wedged between white-fellas and 'primitive people', as he called them, lumping Aborigines and Islanders together.

Occasionally Jim would speak – commendingly – of the reverend Edgar Wells, of Yirrkala mission. Wells, unlike some missionaries, encouraged the local people in their creative art. My father came along, was happy to do some voluntary teaching at the technical school, and introduced some system in the mission's art production. He devised a way of both encouraging talent and rewarding it on a sliding scale. At the same time he provided a steady, major outlet for the broader range of art produced. It is not surprising that in north-east Arnhem Land he enjoyed a high reputation.

Jim understood the connection the art had with dances and ceremonies, and that it was seen as establishing a link between 'the spiritual world of the ancestral beings who created the land, and the living clan members'. So he was always concerned to document the art as fully as possible, to the point where he won the respect of the rising anthropologist and bark-painting specialist Howard Morphy. Jim had a rare capacity to be dispassionate and objective in his appraisals, while being enthusiastic about the art. He was 'almost selfless', Morphy recalls; for him it was a hobby, rather than a business.

In fact it was both. Jim advanced on a broad front, as both a collector and a businessman: he put into practice his own version of Cecil Rhodes' precept, 'philanthropy – and five per cent'. In addition to selling bark paintings to the national galleries in Melbourne and Canberra, he gave them a significant number of paintings outright. But this was less generous than it seemed. At that time an early arts taxation incentive scheme worked by getting the object assessed by two or three valuers, who would arrive at a market value; this could then be claimed in full. The tax deduction was very useful, once placed against the income from Jim's various investments. Besides, bark paintings hanging in galleries with his name as the donor gave him standing – itself commercially useful.

There were definite limits to Jim's public-spiritedness. He tried to get Howard Morphy, who had earmarked a couple of particularly good barks he had for the National Gallery of Australia, to sell them to him instead. And said he would pay more. Meanwhile his accountant despaired, saying he did not price or market his art as effectively as he could have. He didn't seem to want to; 'He kept it all for himself'. Indeed. Barks were the palisades of Jim's walled-in world.

Traditional was kosher, the only way. He was *opposed* to sand paintings of the Papunya school, when around 1980 I alerted him to their existence. The traditional and the static were what appealed. Everything else was a threat – and, as a departure from the legitimated primitive – wrong. He wouldn't see that producing barks as saleable artefacts was itself an adaptation. At the same time, his all-enveloping role as both collector and businessman in practice worked to impede any idea of relinquishment. Once, while living in Canberra, I came across four or five postcards in the National Gallery of barks they had bought from him, duly credited. I proposed to send them to Jim, one by one. But when I saw him after the first one arrived, the dinner table became the site of a headmaster's interrogation. He behaved as though he still owned the paintings, that the Gallery had infringed his control over them, and that somehow I was complicit in all this. I didn't send any more.

WE MUST GO BACK A FRACTION: TO 1969, AND THE NINE months I spent in Melbourne between returning from South Africa and going to England. On my first extended visit (Dad's birthday), there were the two boys: Garry, now rising eight, and Hank, seven. When I'd last seen them, they were too small to register that I would be going away for a long time. I was glad to see how they'd come on: from South Africa, I'd sent lots of postcards with wild animals on them. Now, at the dining table, they held centre stage. But Eve, always corrected or chastised by Jim, said amazingly little; I was brought up sharply by this tacit evidence of his constant battery. To me Eve was perfectly friendly, though more definite. But she had retreated to her room, happy in her own company. There she would play her music – always symphonic, no voices. A Pisces, music served as water for this fish, as she wove in and out, applying the brush to her watercolours. She now painted for pleasure, but I remember thinking that her art had not developed. Emotionally Eve was under-nourished, despite the challenge and love of her two small boys. Jim had rarely mentioned her in his letters. Now when we met, and I asked after her, I got a standard response: 'Ball of muscle!' – fit and functioning. It was true: she never got ill. So eventually – my father's eyes glazing over as his mind wandered off – this tag was stripped down even further: 'Ball o' muss!'

Over the phone, Eve provided despatches from the front.

'Eve! Come here! Quickly!'

Jim had burst into the kitchen. Wondering whatever was wrong, Eve dropped what she was doing and followed him to the main bedroom. There he pointed to the TV. A couple of overturned chairs were lying on their side in front of it. 'Look at that!'

'Look at what?'

'Garry and Hank are trying to trip me up.'

They must have heedlessly run out of the room when a programme ended – in the way of seven- and eight-year-olds.

The kids were developing quickly. Garry was tall and mercurial, with an impressive general knowledge and a good sense of humour. But he had difficulty knuckling down to schoolwork: Jim said he was at the bottom of his class. (Too much discipline at home.) Hank, on the other hand, was pleasant and purposeful, good at sport, and would come to Garry's rescue in schoolyard fights. He had been promoted a grade, and gradually Garry accepted his leadership. After some initial reluctance, he began to play draughts with him. As they sprawled on the carpet near where we sat, Jim would say we should let them play by themselves; not interfere. I agreed. But inevitably there would come a stage when the initiative seemed to have passed to Garry. Father would then begin advising Hank – blatantly, so that I had no choice but to advise Garry. 'No, no!' he'd say. 'We must let them learn the ropes themselves.' I would nod assent, and turn the conversation to another subject. Before long it would become apparent that my audience had switched off.

'No, Garry. Let him have his move again. You must take, Hank.'

'I thought you said you weren't going to interfere.'

'I wasn't. But they must play according to the rules.' I lapse into silence, and look down at the board. Garry moves; he should have taken; it was to his advantage. But my father, also watching, has decided that it's not to his.

IN 1974 I MADE MY SECOND RETURN, FROM ENGLAND. BEFORE long I had found a small flat, a section of an old mansion, in Hawthorn. It was a few minutes' walk from where Olga lived. Perfect: I could keep an eye on her, without her keeping an eye on me. But more often I was visited by Jim. He would come in and relax on the sabre-toothed sofa, as I called it, because of its built-in ashtrays. After my four years away, he seemed pleased that I had returned, and was expansive, friendly. I wasn't so bad after all.

Gradually Jim let drop that a family company had been formed, with Eve and the two boys. One day he said that I should be included in it. I nodded, but fearing a new tool of control, was not wholly enthusiastic. I had enough on my plate with editing *Meanjin*, where the mandate of heaven was passing rather bumpily from Clem Christesen to me. Surprisingly, given Jim's penchant for an implicit pact with other authority figures, he was sympathetic in my difficulties with 'the old bastard'. A few months later I brought up the issue of membership of the company. He told me that it couldn't be done. There was no explanation; none needed, really, as it was 'just a tax device'.

Gradually, the pattern was re-established – as if continuing the old one, from time immemorial – that I would visit my father's house in Cromwell Court, Ravenswood, once every three weeks. Social life there now seemed entirely centred on the gallery: Eve did not entertain, and Jim always preferred to hold the floor. Liveliness at the table came particularly from Garry, who was quick, and effervescent – until stomped on. Hank was quieter, withheld. Much of the conversation when I was there came from Bert, Eve's father. Newly a widower, Bert had gone off to Europe, alone, and systematically seen the sights. A plain man, he had gone to one museum and cathedral after another – since he thought it expected of him – and was miserable.

Meanwhile Jim adopted a customary good neighbour/ bad neighbour policy. On one side were the Carters: Gwen, amusing, personable, with a gaiety about her, and her husband, a pleasant, conventional man who worked in an insurance office. Jim despised him: his slightly whiny voice he made out to be effeminate. He always had some new story about his ineffectuality, compared with his heroic self. On the other side were the Friedmans: Ulla was a professional musician, while Benny had been the first to be friendly. Later, urbane in shorts and with pipe, he would listen to Jim carefully, gently. He could parlay a colonial Hitler, but fell for the propaganda. Years later I saw him at a public gathering, and went up to him: he refused to shake my hand.

Yet they all knew what he was like. One night, the dog belonging to neighbours over the road (who were out) kept barking. About the same time, three people turned up to pacify it: Gwen from next door, with some food, Benny Friedman from the other side, to let it off the chain, and my father, with a gun. He thought of himself as unassailable. Once somebody asked why he didn't get himself a decent car, instead of driving around in a ute. Why? Well, for prestige. 'Prestige!' snorted my father. 'When I get out of my car I take my prestige with me. I don't leave it in the gutter!'

ONE DAY AT *MEANJIN* THE PHONE RANG, AND THE SECRETARY buzzed me: my father on the line. Courtesies exchanged, he came straight to the point.

'About that loan you took from the bank,' he said, 'with me as the guarantor...' He was referring to money I had borrowed to keep me going in England.

'Yes?'

'What's happening about it?'

'It's being repaid. I've paid off $1000 of it.'

'I should have been notified.'

'I didn't think it was necessary. The bank is happy, I am happy, and nearly half the loan is repaid.'

But that wasn't good enough. More followed, which I don't recall. What I do remember is the implacability, the hostility to the point where I said, 'Why are you carrying on like this? You're treating me like an outsider'.

'We haven't treated you like one', he spat out. 'You've made yourself one!'

I then said something dismissive, because I was unprepared for this unprovoked attack at 4 pm on a Friday afternoon, at work.

'Very well. I'll pull the mat from under your feet!'

Click.

There the conversation ended. I thought the weekend would calm him down, but no, the following Monday he contacted the bank manager. He told him he was very ill, could have a heart attack at any time, considered the illness 'quite terminal'. (Superstitious, he had always expected to die at the same age as his father had, sixty-seven, which he had just reached.) Jim asked to be released from the guarantee. But it was not that simple: my approval was required. And I refused to give it.

I wrote a letter to the bank (adopting a high tone) saying that I saw no reason why the existing arrangement should be disturbed. 'There is no possibility', I wrote, that my father would 'become liable for the money out-standing: in the event of my death – a prospect which apparently disturbs him – the debt would, of course, be one of the first legitimate charges upon the estate.'

The bank manager sent the letter on. I allowed a few weeks to pass, and then went to Cromwell Court. Nothing was said, but my father behaved grumpily. I decided I wouldn't go there any more.

Much later, when I had become friendly with the bank manager's successor, he showed me the file. It turned out that the previous April – just after I had produced the first issue of *Meanjin* under my name – my father had approached the bank and told them 'he was sick of his son' who was making 'no attempt to reduce his overdraft', that he had two young sons he would sooner support. He asked the bank to 'lean on [me] heavily'. So it was the old pattern: sending a torpedo to scuttle me just when I looked like steaming ahead, out of reach.

Relations had been no more difficult than usual when he returned to the fray six months later. But gradually I was making a success of the magazine. Perhaps he had been mistaken for me. (It happened.) Perhaps he regarded the recent Papua New Guinea issue as an intrusion upon his territory – with its appearance on Independence Day being an endorsement of a new status that discomfited him. Perhaps he was annoyed by the political stalemate

in Canberra — which would lead ultimately to the Dismissal — and, given the daily irritant of the mounting
crisis, decided to attack the nearest available Whitlamite.
If so, he was acting very much like something he laughed
about: when there was a thunderstorm, Terry the dog
would growl and attack the hose.

WHEN I FINALLY CAME BACK FROM ENGLAND I BEGAN TO
check out the gay scene. Apart from a private gentlemen's
club in Parkville, frequented largely by university graduates
and rather sedate, it was still centred on pubs rather than
nightclubs. The Union Hotel in North Carlton (unfortu-
nately short-lived) was particularly congenial: I recall the
splendid roasts, served at lunch on a wintry Saturday; the
dance floor for later, the perpetual Abba soundtrack, and
the general friendliness. It was so different from England.
I remember a conversation overheard there between two
dons, both gay. It was in Oxford, and one had just been
to a gay bar. 'Anything interesting?' asked the other. 'No',
came the reply. 'Only town,' as distinct from university
types ('gown'). Not worth considering, really.

In central Melbourne, open all day, was the Woolshed
Bar (more correctly, BAA). Below street level, it was
entered by stairs going down from Collins Street. The
bar itself was square; around the perimeter, people sat on
square blocks, in front of a décor of netting, snatches of

wool, and mock kerosene lamps. It had been famous —
notorious — ever since the 1930s, long enough for wide-
eyed country boys or New Zealanders to turn up. Then
there were one or two attracted by its name and décor.
'Jeez, Vern', I heard one bloke say to another, ten minutes
after they sat down, 'the place is full of woolly woofters!'

And so it was. The Woolshed was only a few shops
away from Allan's, I found myself sometimes musing, the
famous old music store where Olga had her first job: she'd
tell of how the council terriers had been let loose once a
month to get rid of rats in the basement. And a generation
earlier — now on to my second Bundy and Coke — Girlie
and Norman would (at street level) have been 'doing the
Block', moving between judges, politicians, businessmen and 'eye-glassed exquisites', promenading fashion-
ably between Swanston and Elizabeth streets. Now their
grandson was in the gully-trap.

The Woolshed was grotty, but the clientele was
extraordinarily mixed, which accounted for its appeal.
First there were the obvious queens, such as Nefertiti,
or the fellow who would turn up dressed in red shirt
and trousers, and a tartan tie — having wrapped himself
up like a Christmas present. Others were more conventional. There would be clerks and salesmen, but also the
odd bohemian, an occasional Aboriginal man, a knot of
deaf-and-dumb people. Sometimes there'd be someone
from the services (the penis, mightier than the sword!).

Or perhaps a troupe of strolling plumbers. Then a dean of law, and the odd outlaw — that's to say someone just out from jail, looking for a helping hand (or whatever). The charms of a few others were available, at a price. One individual, always looking rather serious as he moved purposefully about, had a suspicious lump on his lip: I dubbed him Chancre of the Exchequer. At least once a night a pair of policemen would silently patrol the bar. (Just after one had passed, someone said in a loud, long stage whisper: 'Isn't he beautiful?') The fact was, we were illegals.

There was camaraderie there, when not in direct competition. The Woolshed was, in its funny old way, a refuge: I said to one friend, whom I hadn't seen for a while, 'Here we are again, like battered old trams back at the depot!' The best barmaids recognised that. Once a morose individual looked up and said to one of them, after a long silence, 'I hate fucking poofters!' Annie looked at him squarely, and advised while pulling a beer, 'Well then, you'll just have to stop fucking them, won't you?'

One Saturday evening I had just dropped in at the Woolshed before going to the *Meanjin* office. As I took my position on the tram stop, I was aware of two men I'd noticed earlier running straight towards me. For a split second I thought I should tear off, but there were a lot of people about, so I held my ground. 'Police here', said one, flashing his card. They then said they wanted to question me. I was asked to produce ID. They glanced at my university staff card, saw 'Meanjin Quarterly/Editor', and went into a huddle. (The press.) A sudden restraint: Would I mind coming to the car? I could see no reason not to, so accompanied them around the corner. I was seated in the back; the spokesman turned around and asked if I knew about a particular recent murder. No. Well you see…Jim… Somebody passing has identified you as the murderer. Oh. Would you mind accompanying us to Russell Street? (Even on a Saturday night I would have very much preferred the *Meanjin* office.) Since the claim was so preposterous, and the issue so serious, I thought it best to comply. I was taken to Russell Street: small fluorescent-lit rooms, men in purple shirts, tobacco tins serving as ashtrays. I was asked to give an account of myself: fortunately, for the day in question, I could account for my movements and had witnesses at every stage. Equally fortunate, they did not ask where I had just been. But it did not end there. After a line-up a man came in, paused, then nodded: 'Yes…that's the one!' Right, I said, this has gone far enough. I'm not saying another word until I get a lawyer. It's OK, they assured me, you can go now. (False identification was just a trick, to trigger a confession.) It had been an unpleasant experience. A surreal proposition ran through my mind, since I was due to appear before the Literature Board of the Australia Council to plead the case for *Meanjin*. The magazine might be slaughtered in Sydney while its editor was held on a murder charge in Melbourne.

Running *Meanjin* was a job I liked, for all the difficulties involved in putting out a high cultural magazine
in Australia. I found that the pattern of extended recep-
tivity, as one put out feelers across a wide field in order
to draw in interesting material, followed by the sudden
switch to editorial assertiveness, seemed to suit my temperament. I gained confidence. Instead of a hint of a
stammer, there was a new-found capacity to talk with
people over the phone I'd never met before, extending to
laughter. Thoughts of suicide, which had lingered on in
London (as a rational option, perhaps) disappeared. I had
a strong sense of purpose, sharing the Whitlamite belief in
the importance of developing an Australian high culture.
While Jim's imaginative world still spun on the Fly and
the Ok-Birak, my imagination was fired by Jack Hibberd
and his ocker baroque. More and more I came to see more
conventional academics as being like those boys in class
who always put up their hand and yell out, 'Sir! Sir! Please,
sir!' Only they hadn't noticed that everybody else had got
up and left the room.

As regards my sexuality, I had to be careful at the beginning. As editor of *Meanjin*, I had – and made – enemies.
So rather than proclaiming it, I adopted a policy of
non-denial and gradual disclosure. 'The editor of *Meanjin*
is a poof' would have been a great item of non-news, beating even the smallest earthquake in Chile. But in those
days, when to be anti-gay was still a socially endorsed

prejudice, I had to be wary. And the job created other problems. Because its demands were great, its standards so high and its resources so poor, I often had to cancel social arrangements at short notice. This spelt death for developing relationships. And it was real attachment I sought, not the fleeting encounters of most gay life. I also wanted to move in a wider world than the gay ghetto, which was now taking shape. Some time later, I was at a lunch where Don Dunstan, then living in Melbourne, was the guest of honour. After he left early, one activist remarked, 'I think Don…is having trouble adapting to gay culture'. I couldn't let that one pass. 'Shouldn't that make you wonder, then, about gay culture?'

FROM ONE OR TWO MUTUAL ACQUAINTANCES I RECEIVED word that Jim would like me to visit him. Long after, a postcard arrived, asking that I get in touch. Should this not happen, then…'I accept it'. The message tugged at me; it was the nearest I would get to an apology. I began to feel that I might have proved a point. I had not only been editing *Meanjin*, but was about to produce an Aboriginal issue: Jim would have learned of that through a friend, an arts administrator. And I had, in the interim, bought and moved into a house. Independence had been achieved. So perhaps I could venture out to Cromwell Court, unannounced. (That would be a better test.)

Whether I ever went there again or not would depend on how I was received.

I encountered Eve first. She didn't want to know about the difference with my father. Since he didn't recognise me when he came into the room, she announced me: 'Jim Junior!' Nearly two years had passed. I went up and kissed him. Soon we were seated by ourselves: he asked why I hadn't been to see him for so long. I told him that he had always seemed to have difficulty in accepting my right to a separate, individual personality without feeling threatened, without it necessitating a complete break. He listened, in acceptance. But when I moved on to two things in particular that had bugged me about the last visit, he mobilised immediately. A particular photo I'd requested had been lost (though he hadn't said so, then); and as for Garry coming to see me (the expression which crossed his face when I had suggested it told me it would never happen), well, Garry was an individual, and he'd have to make up his own mind...Always an answer, always the ability to put you in the wrong.

Had I been a tactician, I would have proposed this meeting on neutral ground. But my claim on him – and on them all – was that of family. It had to be Cromwell Court. Perhaps weakly, I passed over the basic affront, his behaviour over the loan guarantee: I had checkmated him at the time. So to these lesser points I simply nodded.

'He has aged,' I noted at the time. 'His skull is more

prominent – a grey Montgolfier balloon, straining at the ropes. His voice is lighter, fluffier. And he's lost weight, two whole stones of it. He's become a diabetic. For all that he seems well…as I told him. He agreed (something he'd have never admitted in the past). The seventies have been much kinder to him than the sixties, and that was thoroughly unexpected.'

Gradually the others joined us. The tone was one of quiet friendliness: compared with the heat of the day outside, it was almost a sombre tableau of the Prodigal Son. Suddenly I felt that I was with my own kind – an odd feeling, for one so solitary. There he was, talking of Arnhem Land, of spending a couple of hours with Xavier Herbert near Cairns, still reading the papers fiercely, still forcefully seeking the broad trend (often wrong-headedly, always anti-Labor). And I realised – despite everything – how much I owed him.

A FEW MONTHS AFTERWARDS, I SAID TO EVE THAT I WAS getting on well with him. He hasn't really changed, she said over the phone; he's just being cautious with you. Even so, there were surprises. One day he suddenly proposed we should go to South Africa together. I pointed out that, being underpaid, I would need some help if this were to happen. That was the last I heard of it. (It was just as well: he would have wanted to plug into my networks, and generally have me act as caddy.) And around this time, as one day we sat together in the lounge, he suddenly asked, 'What are your little problems?' It was something he'd never asked before. 'They're not little to me', I replied. He inquired no further.

But once he was pressing, after a meal, that I should accompany him on a visit to a factory he owned. I detected some urgency about this, so went along. His plaint, as it turned out, was one of loneliness. He had thought, as old friends disappeared, he would be able to make new ones. Not so. 'The New Guinea friends' – he named them – 'and nearly everyone in Tassie, is dead'. Arnhem Land was the great compensation…but the doctor wasn't keen on him going there, saying he might die. 'I wouldn't mind dying up there', he added quietly. 'They'd give me a real send-off. They said they would.'

Soon the conversation was turned into an attack on Garry: it was hard having a builder's apprentice in a professional home, he said. I was shocked; I had never heard him use the language of class before. But here it was, stiffening domestic antagonisms. Rough as bags, he said, and it fell upon him to keep him up to the mark: Eve didn't mind, for she came from a tradesman's home. She was used to it. As for Hank – he had already hinted that he was steadier, a student, would take over the business. Not that he said that with any great enthusiasm – but Hank had shown some interest in Aboriginal artefacts. Not long after, as we stood waiting together on a tram stop, Jim began to run him down. The one-time favourite was now seen to be a public servant type – a terrible thing. Jim saw only his guardedness, his caution. I tried to reassure him. Be patient: each son will take different things from you, and build on them. I've taken your sense of the world, your love of the distinctiveness of far-away places. (Hank developed a taste for the wilderness.) But he would have none of it. At that stage he could only see something wrong with each of us.

And, increasingly, with Eve. How she was just a 'Bush Kanaka' (Bougainville bogan gets it), an incompetent out of her depth. It has to be said, as a preliminary, that he had never lost his taste for having black servants: at Monash Avenue, when looking for his keys, he would joke about having a special 'key boy'. The swing door into the kitchen from the L-shaped room emphasised its domestic focus: any exit meant that Eve went back to where she belonged, back into the servants' quarters.

It was getting her down; she was much more serious in demeanour, now. Once – he must have been away – she came to my house by herself, to talk things over. I did my best to be encouraging. Occasional letters came too, when I was away. Then, since she usually picked up the phone when I rang my father's, I began to have lengthening conversations with her, before being put on to Jim. Similarly, since the front door was unlocked when I was expected, I would go into the kitchen first for a conversation, before he appeared. I'd be listening, cheering her up; hers was often a weary humour about the impossibility of it all. She would always carefully change the subject the moment Jim came through the swing door. One day I suggested to Eve that she needn't bother: all we had to do was to stop talking and look at him inquiringly – he would think that perfectly natural. It worked.

Every three weeks or so Eve would put on a family dinner. Garry and Hank did most of the talking, as they put school behind them and began to face up to the world. Hank was increasingly assertive, flexing his muscles; Garry voluble, coming at things in a rush. Eve would playfully make a remark or two to one or the other, or both, or me – my father meanwhile dominating by complaining (to Eve), or being corrective. Significantly, he wasn't generally addressed by name. Out of hearing Garry and Hank, and later Eve, had come to call him SJ (with a nice touch of satire) – Super Jim. I was still comfortable calling him Dad; it seemed odd to be uttering my own name to someone across the table, and the old endearment was a quiet assertion of a basic tie. Meanwhile he never let go. One day, as we sat down to dinner, Eve and I (seated next to each other) looked out over the valley. 'A haunting sunset', she commented. I agreed; nice tonalities. Suddenly my father turned round, to glance at the view. 'That's not a sunset', he declared in a loud voice. 'In

Central Australia you'll see a *real* sunset. A man's sunset!'

Once, at the dinner table, I picked up a disparaging remark Garry made about the Aborigines, and land rights. Probing him further, I came up against the hard line. I turned to Jim: 'But you're pro-Aboriginal. You must be for them.' He said nothing. When I said what being opposed meant, and that people should resist the trampling on Aboriginal rights in all sorts of ways, I just got a cryptic, gloating smile. It was a shock: I'd written to the paper from England in 1971 in support of land rights, and Jim was pleased. But that was then. *Whitlam* had come to power since, while young blacks had taken over the Aboriginal Advancement League. And although his friend Edgar Wells was opposing the mining companies as vigorously as he could, Jim kept his nose clean. His interest in Aboriginal people was not advocatorial. To some extent he made an exception for Yirrkala: the people there were *real* Aborigines. But when the chips were down, Jim's Aboriginal interest was the old paternalism in new guise.

His authority was asserted at every opportunity. 'I know Bob Hawke!' he protested in argument one day. Eve would have none of it. 'That [fleeting encounter] was thirty years ago!' she declared. It was a plea for significance, for being a personage. Hence the *delight* with which he told the story of a Papuan who had been hanged – he had imperilled a white man in some way, innocently. It was a matter of 'face', Jim said. The correct social order had to be restored: the incident was narrated with great self-satisfaction, as if demonstrating an elegant equation. More frequently he upheld his position through pedantry. Once he was particularly emphatic about the pronunciation of the name of a Melbourne organist – but not being an expert in Dutch or Frisian, I kept out of it.

Not surprisingly, at table there wasn't much room for wit. Dangerous. Too playful. They preferred jokes: Hank told one about two macho mice, outdone by a third, who wanted to screw the cat. On another occasion the subject of swearing came up. Eve said she thought it would die out, as words lost their potency. Jim said nothing – in fact, like a lot of men of his generation, he swore sparingly.

'Oh I don't know', I said. 'People will invent new ones.'

'Will they?' asked Eve.

'Yes. They already have. Words like…brown-nose… cocksucker…', and, later, 'motherfucker'.

She was unfamiliar with them. I had to explain what brown-nosing was. Around the table there was a tense silence. 'I reckon one day they will be exhausted from over-use too, and people will then have to invent a fresh lot…If you repeat swear words often enough', I added, 'they lose their power'.

Eve paused. There was a gleam in her eye. 'Brown-nose, cocksucker, motherfucker', she began, slowly. 'Brown-nose, cocksucker, motherfucker. Brown-nose, cocks—'

'Eve! Stop it! Stop it!'

WHAT I WAS INCREASINGLY AWARE OF, AS I SAT AROUND THAT table, was that a kind of sibling rivalry had been thrust upon me. It had come too late, and I was unprepared for it. They were not interested in my world. The old high culture had entered its decline, or at least its relegation. Moreover, as I was nearing fifty, I realised that I seemed to be fighting a new set of battles with my father. Had nothing been won, or conceded, when I voluntarily came back to the fold? It seemed not.

Jim still saw himself as being the central figure in the life of each family member. He therefore continued to appropriate whatever he fancied. If I took him to a restaurant, I might turn up later and find him, having taken people there himself. Similarly, when I asked whether he'd received a copy of a book I'd produced from the publishers, he said, 'Yes. They knew to do the right thing'. It did not occur to him that they sent it because I asked them to. But that assumption was mild, compared with other controlling behaviour. Having – in one of those rare acts of encouragement he allowed himself from time to time – come to a *Meanjin* conference I held, comparing Sydney and Melbourne, and seen it was a conspicuous success – he then felt compelled to undercut me. (Perhaps I had not sufficiently acknowledged my traditional owner.) I had gone almost immediately to England, France and Monaco, to begin my research for the book *Lyrebird Rising*. He went into hospital, and told Eve I should be brought home. She remonstrated with him: there wasn't much I could do, and it would completely muck up my plans. That, of course, was intended: it was an assertion of authority at the moment I was showing not only independence, but confirming a different identity. It was as though I had captured the name Jim Davidson and run off with it. I must be tackled and, if possible, brought down. He had already found that he had to differentiate himself from me, in his rare publications, as 'James A Davidson'. He would not have been happy about it.

But his hand lay even heavier on the other two, growing-up sons. Once Garry went off on an expedition to the Grampians, with a couple of friends. He had probably been told to phone at some point, and when he didn't – it was the kind of thing he could be lax about – my father got in touch with the police. There was a full search: they found him. Garry later did not want to talk about it. There was a similar incident with Hank. My father found that when working in outback New South Wales, he had applied for a driving licence and got it. In that state you could get one a year earlier than Victoria, and so Hank was driving about Melbourne in a state of quasi-legality. He must have annoyed Jim about something, for my father got in touch with the local police station. They told him they weren't interested. But I was: what an insight into the psychology of an informer, as in Nazi Germany! And how right I had been, in those long years of illegality, to be buttoned up about my homosexuality. How he would have loved to trigger the punitive drama of shock treatment, or even imprisonment – although there he might have been held back by a sense of being shamed.

I had been back from Canberra almost a year when Hank also returned. Characteristically, Jim had engineered a crisis, which had resulted in a stand-off between them, a few months after I went up to the ANU. I was called upon to solve it. I said I would do my best, but don't ask me to intervene again. They were reconciled, and now Hank was very much in evidence at the Court – a young man with a frown. For Eve he had always been the favourite: the unexpected child, the gift, in peril in his early years from bad attacks of croup. He would provide her with moral support, and embolden her. She learned to drive, played the stock market, once went overseas. In return, Eve adoringly endorsed his various schemes. It was the time of Gordon Gekko's mantra, 'Greed is good!' And Hank had the perfect response, should anything be questioned: 'It's in the genes!' he'd declare. It was hard to quarrel with that.

Occasionally dinners for my father's birthday were held at a businessmen's haunt in Fairfield – a crooner and a musician or two came with the neo-American food: the Playboy Club, without the bunnies. And gradually it came about that I would hold a midwinter occasion, for a joint celebration of my birthday and Garry's at my place. The old kitchen, with its cheerful fire, was then at its best; Eve never failed to admire the reflection of red tulips in the windows. Outright dramas were avoided, but my father would still attempt to rule the roost. Once, when I was crisply explaining a current political impasse involving the Greens in Tasmania, he piped up: 'This is boring!' Although they'd been listening, no-one else said a thing. If I'd replied, 'You're in my house now. You'll just have to put up with it', he would have been quite capable of saying, 'C'mon, Eve, let's get out of here'. And left, expecting me to make an apologetic phone call the next day. On another occasion Dad and Eve were unable to come. I chatted with Garry and his girlfriend amiably, but Hank was eager to dominate. He spoke of the way he was determined, through exercise, to 'build up my aggression', and then gave me, as part of my present, a record of Daddy Cool. Knowing that neither the music nor the title would appeal to me – each clinching the other – he let out a chuckle.

There were, for a time, also unexpected visits by Jim. He developed the habit of parking nearby, and would knock on the door. Could I let him use the toilet? After this happened two or three times, it became plainer that that was it, finito. He would never stop for a drink or have a chat: 'Must be off, Jim!' This was getting on my wick. So one day when he followed this routine, he suddenly heard a strange, insistent noise. I was tapping a coin on a plate: a trick I had learned when trying to off-load a Monégasque ten-franc coin at a public loo in the Paris Metro. It made an incredible din, and was the way the grim-faced woman in attendance had called me back to pay the right money. Now it disconcerted him, too – so much so that a few days later a letter arrived, containing a fifty-dollar bill.

BUT AROUND THIS TIME THERE WAS A DRAMATIC SHIFT IN context.

I remember thinking that if *Don Giovanni* were retold in a contemporary setting, it might involve not the flames of hell but the steam of a gay sauna. Who knew what could be incubating there? Some months later, just as the Canberra bus was doing its enormous loop on to Commonwealth Bridge, I read in the paper of a mysterious disease that had appeared in America: in Australia the first patient had just presented with the same symptoms. I didn't give it much attention. But six months later it was another story.

AIDS had burst upon us. So little was known about it: how it was caught, how long the incubation period, and what proportion of HIV+ people would seroconvert to 'full-blown AIDS'. Except in Africa, where the disease was stubbornly heterosexual, the susceptible categories were homosexuals, intravenous drug users, haemophiliacs – and Haitians. As the American comedian Mort Sahl said, 'The worst thing about AIDS is…trying to convince your parents that you're Haitian'. The medics could have done with some convincing too – or at least consultation with sociologists and historians. There was no real mystery: French-speaking Haitian professionals had gone to Francophone Africa, had early exposure to the disease, and then brought it back. But ignorance was still fairly general. Late in 1983 a Canberra doctor, recently returned from spending a few professional months in San Francisco, told a large audience of gay men that, 'You have as much chance of dying from AIDS as of being kicked to death by a duck'. Relief filled the hall with laughter.

A gay culture had only just emerged, based on the gym as much as the bar. Hardness could be achieved not only through team sports; the clone, too, was an emphatic rejection of the image of the cissy. Around this time I ran across a friend in a gay bar, a painter, just returned from overseas. Doomed, he said, as we strolled from the partying in one room to another. All doomed. Other people, as the marginalised have often done, could lapse into a grim, easy fatalism. We'll all get it…may as well.

Then, just as relations with my father were becoming difficult, television screens exploded with the image of the Grim Reaper. AIDS as death in a bowling alley – knocking down people like ten-pins. It was a public health campaign, so effective that it induced hysteria. At least it wasn't as bad as America, where Christian chundermentalists were urging people to 'Kill a Queer for Christ!'

AIDS, and the extra stigma gayness now acquired, was the last thing I needed.

TENSION HAD BEEN BUILDING FOR SOME TIME. SOME WEEKS after it was held, I mentioned to Eve that my midwinter dinner had gone well. She scoffed. It went well because... that afternoon SJ had asked her to do some potting. When he came out to 'supervise', he found it hadn't been done to his satisfaction. She 'would never learn', was 'a silly bitch', and so on. Eve said she would not stand for this...As she moved off, my father in response kicked the pots away. Once inside the house, Eve gave him no further thought. She began wrapping a parcel. Suddenly there he was in front of her, silent and menacing, a certain glint in his eye...He grabbed her and hauled her to the sofa, abusing her and saying he would kill her. Eve went quiet on him – too afraid to speak. He let go. She then went outside; fortunately Hank was visiting, and could be summoned to go on patrol, and pacify his father. So the 'success' of my dinner had been partly reactive.

A few months later came the twenty-ninth anniversary of their first going out together. Eve showed me a letter she had written him. She outlined what she had brought to the marriage, recognised as a partnership shaped by him. Yes, it had prospered – with investment properties, and Aboriginal art. But she took offence at the way he always described the collection as 'his' – reminding him that together they had brought four paintings back from Central Australia, and had built the business up from that, always ploughing the profits back. That was the case for many years, until their partnership (in this) was put on a legal basis. She hadn't cared then under whose name it had been placed, because she trusted him. Eve drew attention to all the effort she had made in helping to mount the exhibitions, among other things. And what had she received for it? A cheque for $1000.

She asked him, 'What was that for, exactly?'

'Your work', he replied.

'You think it's only a matter of money, don't you?'

It seems he replied, Yes. She then tore up the cheque (so she said to me), rather than be bought off so easily.

Not so long after, at the dinner table with a young woman setting out as an Aboriginal art dealer, Eve questioned my father's ascription of a painting to a particular artist: she knew from another reproduction that it wasn't. 'I'll get into hot water afterwards', she joked. For a day or two there was no trouble – then out it came, as it often did, all the sharper for the incubation: 'By the way…', he began. Never correct him in front of others; that had been a 'private' conversation. Since – apart from anything else – Eve had been sitting down at the meal she had placed upon the table, she challenged him. But he told her she knew nothing – couldn't pronounce the names properly –

was setting herself up as an 'expert'. Again the glint in the eye: 'I'll kill you, and I'll kill myself too', he declared. But thinking better of it, he fell to the floor, feigning a heart attack. He himself later said to Garry – not realising how revealing it was – that it was as with Olga, all over again.

And yes, Eve fled the house. It was early morning: she hadn't got properly dressed. Throwing a rug over herself from the back of her car, she went in to the new neighbours next door. The wife gave her some clothes. They went outside, and there was Jim: they announced that Eve was going with them to Olinda for the day. He was surprised, expected to be invited, but then fell in with it. 'Good idea', he said, and moved off. In a way Eve was relieved to see him, to know that he was not ailing but up and about.

When they returned, Eve felt she could not go home. Then she remembered that Hank had said there'd be nobody in his shared house that weekend. So she made her way there, not taking her car: the engine starting up would have alerted Jim. In fact one of Hank's housemates was home, 'entertaining'. Assuring her that she would keep out of her way, Eve went up to Hank's room. She laughed, as she wondered what he would think should he come home to find his mother asleep on his bed. ('Every son's dream!' said I.) When he returned, Hank decided to go over to Cromwell Court and tap on Garry's window, telling him what had happened. Garry came over the next day; he suggested to Eve that she should lie low. Jim would do anything to get her back.

That wasn't quite how it played out. It was true for the first day; but on the second he was speaking of divorce. ('I've news for you, Jim', said Garry. 'This is 1987.' He seemed to have no idea that his assets would be divided.) There was some wild talk of going into a home, since he always imagined that there he would be waited on hand and foot. But on the third day, he was talking of getting a Fijian or Papua New Guinean exchange student. 'They're more obedient', he said. But they would have to study, said Garry. He would tell them when they could study, said Jim. It seems he got as far as making a phone call to the Fijian Association.

Eve would return, but first I was told by Jim that there would be a family 'conference'. As I was not directly involved, it was no particular surprise that I wasn't invited. Hank told me something of the discussion: Eve's meagre allowance had to be increased, in addition to the payment of a lump sum; and she must be able to go away for two or three days each month. Jim apparently wasn't very keen on that idea, and both Hank and I thought there would be backsliding. It was hard, with a man like that, to get any terms to stick: the very imposition of them was always taken as an affront, not an agreement. Meanwhile he could take it out on me. I'd promised to take him to *HMS Pinafore* (which I'd reviewed). First there was cavilling about dates, and then the tickets had to be changed, as he wanted an aisle seat so that he could extend his leg. It turned out that I had placed him in the wrong aisle; different leg, this time. He said I would have to change the tickets again. That I refused to do. He would have to change them himself, and – as a deadline had suddenly cropped up – instead of me, go with Eve. The jollity would have been entirely on the stage.

The 'conference' seems, in retrospect, to have bolted the family together. SJ now found that he had two grown sons who would come to the defence of their mother. And Hank, who was closest to her, was the one in whom he now placed most confidence. Hank became company secretary of the commodified family. For a time he proposed to follow a long trip overseas with a job in Hong Kong, but then realised the home front needed close monitoring. Meanwhile Garry was planning a strategic withdrawal. He was now doing up a house he had bought with Jim in a neighbouring suburb: the inevitable rows had resulted in his buying out his father, as he intended to live there. A new girlfriend, Susie, made her appearance: they became engaged, and would marry. Meanwhile concentrating on his trade suited him perfectly: that way Garry could express his ingenuity, and enjoy independence. He was sick of being the Household Cavalry. Once, when he was sleeping in after having gone to a party, Jim told him to get up – or he would sue him. And then there was the evening Jim alerted him to the fact that he might require him to donate a kidney: Father's sole surviving one was weakening. Head office was in trouble; one of the branches might have to shut down, if necessary. Garry decided to hop it.

I was horrified when I went over to see them around this time and found there was an intercom in the kitchen: Eve could now be summoned to the bedroom as Jim pleased. ('That voice!' she said. 'I think I'll hear it to the end of my days!') The ratchet seemed to be tightening. He got himself a powerful portable phone, capable of picking up calls and monitoring them, for a distance of up to eight houses away. Previously Eve had felt safe speaking frankly when he was in the garden. Since there was always a drama when she wanted to use the phone – notes would be thrust under her nose, saying there was an 'important' call he was waiting on – she got (in those days before mobiles) a landline of her own. Later, when I again went overseas, she wrote me a couple of letters: her fear was that, as I moved on, one of them might be returned to sender – and then intercepted and read by him. The poor woman, believing it to be obligatory to fill in the sender details, fudged her name and the address.

It was not as if these developments could be viewed simply as irksome restraints. Eve was finding she could no longer converse with my father. Her opinions were always dismissed, and when she expressed them she was accused of starting an argument. She wasn't allowed to see the newspaper until he was ready to hand it over; the *Art Bulletin* she wasn't allowed to see at all, because 'it's mine'. And anything could produce a new crisis. Once she went into his office to turn on the heater an hour before he returned. That only brought down his wrath: she had violated the inner sanctum. There was constant abuse, and threats – she knew nothing (she had borrowed from the bank for shares and lost money in the 1987 crash), was a silly bitch, he would bash her brains in. Small wonder that she drifted about in a low-level depression. 'There are the mini-melodramas', she wrote to me overseas. 'They, like the poor, are always with one. From lost glasses, car keys and stolen biros to all the real and imagined problems that only the flesh of SJ could possibly be heir to. I'm sure a global disaster and a missed weather report are equally major. I'm certain I've lost the ability to react to either.'

Jim, meanwhile, had become more inclined to follow current events, but always from an alarmist perspective. There had been a day when he was relatively open. At a time of tension with Indonesia over what was then Dutch New Guinea, he had gone along to a talk given by the Indonesian foreign minister, Dr Subandrio. In the mid-1960s he even said he didn't mind paying more tax, since it meant he was making more money. But by the 1980s he had changed completely. He was now proud of the fact that, as he put it in an interview, he was 'independently wealthy'. Then at one stage, after some border incident in Papua New Guinea, he wanted to give the Liberal party information about the area. He had no notion of bipartisanship, of abiding national interests, of the officials of DFAT – he just wanted to give the Liberals what he saw as ammunition against Labor. He dropped hints that he was involved in the 'Joh for Canberra' campaign of 1987, when Queensland's right-wing premier almost wrecked the Liberal party in a clumsy lunge for power. Jim had gone so far to the right he was wrong. He may have been the only man in Australia who described Bob Hawke as a Communist.

There were – and would continue to be – my father's medical emergencies, periods in hospital, 'ops'. Once the three of them (I had not been told) were in a waiting room, and discussed why they felt so detached, so little involved. He had worn them out. Eve had said that she now regarded him 'purely as a task': as a professional problem, I suggested. Yes. She would submit to that extent for the sake of her children, was the unspoken assumption. Even so, she would find it necessary to abandon house again.

When driving me home one day Hank expressed his concern about SJ's treatment of Eve. There was some wild talk. At different times we had all felt like this. 'Anyway', said Hank, 'I don't think it will go on for much longer.'

'Oh I don't know', I said. 'I reckon he'll still be alive in…three years.'

'Oh no!'

'Well, he's tough… Tell you what', I said, with a touch of devilment. 'Let's bet on it.'

'Wickedness!' Hank said gleefully, as we shook hands – the favourite son and the black sheep. Dadda's extension of life was deemed to be worth ten dollars. Time passed, and Jim sailed on past the three-year limit. I won the bet – but never saw the money.

THEN THERE WAS CHRISTMAS. IT RARELY PASSED WITHOUT incident. Eve placed great store on it, and, in addition to preparing the dinner, made every effort to make it the one day of the year. While Jim just gave banknotes, the rest of us discussed what the presents should be. There was good sense in this: no point in someone with different tastes spending money on something not wanted. So booty was exchanged for plunder. To restore a sense of the unexpected, Eve came up with the idea of a 'mini' (present), which we also gave each other. Garry had apparently been wondering what ornamentation he might put on a redesigned section of his garden, so found himself the proud possessor of a hideous clay fish. Recycled wrapping paper was the thing, because it gave rise to tired old jokes about saving money. One year I gave my presents entirely patch-wrapped in it: Eve took a dim view of this. I was sending them up.

The day began, at Cromwell Court, with Eve preparing the dinner while Jim went off to have Christmas drinks with Binny Lum, a onetime radio personality. At one stage she must have made a fuss of him, and invited him to Christmas drinks; he kept on going ever after. Once I went, too: a bored young man from Adelaide was surprised, and asked why I'd come. 'On Christmas Day', I replied, 'I'm a self-governing dominion within the Empire.'

Then back to the house. The L-shaped room was bedecked with strung-up Christmas cards; an impressive display, until you looked carefully and saw that many of them were old ones. Jim meanwhile would push the swing door and go through to the kitchen. He would 'supervise' – if necessary adding salt to the gravy, to (his) taste. Then he would start to get impatient. Once, having first gone by train, as I usually did, to see Olga in the home in Brighton where she now lived, I was a bit late. Jim knew that I had to catch two more trains operating on a restricted time-table, but it made no difference. He insisted on starting the dinner without me. There was neither welcome nor apology when I arrived. I decided, seeing them tucking in, Fuck this! Returning to where I'd placed the presents, I then went back to the table, and hurled them at the family as they ate. I stormed out. (Perhaps the musket rattled.) Then I took to my heels and ran, to distance myself. Suddenly I stopped, and burst into laughter. The absurdity of it all! Eventually I talked to Jim on the phone. He spoke with puzzlement about my behaviour, but his mannered voice told me this was completely manufactured.

At another Christmas, having snitched at Eve, he suddenly decided he'd had enough of compulsory goodwill – it was a strain coping with his three grown-up sons all together, set in intricate family relationships he couldn't quite control. He felt 'sat on'. Besides, the stock exchange was closed, exasperatingly – so Jim strode off into the garden, and to the incinerator. He wouldn't celebrate the Lord's day; rather, he had sloped off to stoke the fires of hell.

Jim would have already collected his loot. Eve had learned, the hard way, that he should be given his presents first. (This also kept him occupied while other people were receiving theirs.) Although instructed to always check with him first regarding the choice of present, I decided to go in for a game of skill, giving him something that he really liked but hadn't thought of. One time I couldn't help myself. I gave Jim a book of interviews, called *Taim [Time] Bilong Masta*. He peered at it, so I told him what it was, a book about whitefella bosses in New Guinea. Then added for the others, pointing to the title, 'It's a book about eternity!'

EVE HAD BECOME LESS AND LESS HAPPY ABOUT GOING OUT with him. So to some extent I filled the breach, at least as far as films were concerned. Once I went with him to see Paul Cox's film about van Gogh, *Vincent*. When we went into the cinema, he sat down immediately in front of the only two other people there. Then he started complaining, in a loud voice, about a man in one of his factories giving him trouble. They got up and moved; I had to signal an apology. The film began, and I became absorbed in the images and in Vincent's correspondence with his brother. I was aware of Jim watching me; the emotional landscape of the letters was completely dead for him.

Meanwhile he would ring from time to time, nearly always with purpose. Could I advise on a copyright question? Get hold of a book for him? Suggest where a friend could find a ghostwriter? At times he could be rude, even then. But the worst was when I rang him. When I began by asking him how he was, he'd always say, 'Bloody lousy!' 'Oh', I was tempted to reply, 'and what particular form does the lousiness take today?' (Hank said he never asked.) Commiseration would nearly always be followed by, 'I can't talk to you now, Jim.' It seemed I always picked a deuce of a time to ring. Once he was so brisk with this routine that I rang back immediately after, insisting on the right to hold a conversation. He retreated into expressed and simulated exhaustion.

There was this distancing, and also a manoeuvring around the old man. I had forgotten that, when I'd turned up again unexpectedly after an absence of two years,

Eve looked put out. She was one who held on to hidden resentments, and had a punitive streak. Once, when I said I was going to Banyule – then an art gallery – and would walk from Heidelberg station, she said I should take a cut lunch. I looked at her questioningly. 'You'd better get used to it', she said. Much later, as a 'mini', she gave me a wad of postage stamps. I looked at them askance – I claimed half the ones I used as a tax deduction – and was told that one day I'd be grateful. These cryptic remarks I preferred not to hear: they were so fleeting I did not take them as revealing a deep intent. After all, we got on well.

But they went with something else. When I pointed out how, when I went away, Jim had always manufactured a crisis to exert control, she was not convinced. Eve rarely discussed the past – in any way – and would not see how it could linger, influencing behaviour and projecting recurring patterns. In fact there was a great deal she refused to see. One day I was surprised to hear her refer to the air crash Jim was involved in. The air crash? Yes, the one in 1934. It was the first I'd heard of it. My mother always called it 'the accident', I told her, and the common understanding of the term then was a road accident. Eve refused to take this on board, and sent Garry into the State Library (where he had sometimes gone to follow up shipping history) to look up the newspapers. Incredible! All the time wasted searching for an air crash that never happened!. Then, when next in Tasmania, I decided to ask Jim's old girlfriend Gwen. Immediately she burst into laughter. 'He was on a motor bike', she said, 'and ran into a fruit truck full of cabbages'.

MY FATHER'S TACTICS TOWARDS ME VARIED FROM TIME TO time. Once in a while, instead of an exocet phone call (the British had just used those missiles to devastating effect in the Falklands War), there could be a real sweetener. One New Year's Day he turned up, with some home-grown tomatoes, and chatted for a couple of hours, quite genially. That time there was no kick-back. But often any sudden affinity between us would be undercut by some fresh act of hostility. It was as if, from his private Olympus of money and power, he was restoring a sense of his own integrity, satisfying a primal need to remain uncompromised.

At best, my sexuality was a disappointment to him — 'It's a damned shame', he said once. Since I could not satisfy his deepest, very normal expectations, I was damaged goods. Why ever would anyone voluntarily renounce Man's Estate? — for so he would have seen it. In doing so, I had broken an implicit contract. As I began to sense the drift of things regarding inheritance, I once asked why I should be excluded. 'You know why', he replied.

But one day he rang to say that he was giving me $1000 — on condition that I used it towards paying off my housing loan. I had no objection to that. The cheque arrived, and I banked it accordingly. A few days later he rang again, this time to offer another $6000. Clearly he had been in touch with the bank manager to see if I had done as he had bid, before paying the additional sum: 'It has nothing to do with them', he said, as if thinking aloud. 'It comes from the sale of my art collection, and so is my own money'. This time he deposited it.

I did not realise it at the time, but this was the grand overture to a series of manoeuvres. He had always been concerned about wills, and when I turned twenty-one insisted I make one. (The fact that I wanted to leave my books and records – the only things I had of much value – to particular friends, rather than to himself, annoyed him.) More recently, talking about his own, it was evident that from time to time he would adjust precisely what I would inherit. (Almost like a quotation on the stock exchange, really.) It was never very much: people deemed no longer fit for purpose were basically discarded. He did say, at one point, that he was impressed by the way I had continued to look after Olga. In other words, I had taken her off his hands; she was my responsibility now.

Eighteen months or so after giving me money towards paying off the house, it turned out to have been a sleeper. One day Jim rang, in exocet style, to ask what was I doing with it, since *he* was drawing up a new will. Was I leaving the house to the family? There was no articulated proposition. Instinctively I felt that a bird in hand was worth two in the bush – and said No. That brought the conversation to an abrupt end. It did not stop him, when he came over, saying 'You should sell the house' a couple of times, or raise money on it, to buy further property. He never got it that I did not consider money-making the prime purpose of life. When, as the result of an advance on a book, I said I had to pay provisional tax, his response was a diatribe against the socialist government – and the advice to form a shelf company, as Hank and Garry had done.

He asked about superannuation: I had little. So he said he would talk to his accountant: he'd tried, he said, to get me a percentage of the income from the company, but these things were difficult, and it couldn't be done. (There was nothing in the articles of association, I later learned, that precluded it.) And so he suggested that he purchase an annuity for me. I wasn't keen on this idea: the amount would be low, I knew, and the insurance company would require me to take a blood test. Because of AIDS, I did not want to do that. I didn't want to know whether I had it. Moreover, if I were found to be HIV+, then that would immediately restrict travel: a growing number of countries wouldn't admit people who were seropositive. And since there was no cure, and little treatment then, there was no advantage in finding out. I had already decided not to have sex (then), so could not infect others. I would take what might come if I had to, but – since I had enough problems at the time – would prefer not to be spooked by the fact that it was coming.

Some months later, by arrangement, Jim came to my house. 'Eleven o'clock?' I said, letting him in, for – unusually – he was late. 'It's OK, it's just that I have to catch a plane to Canberra at two.' We went into the kitchen. He made for his usual side of the big table, but I stopped him. Today would be different. An indication was the files and documents placed on that side of the table, which I now occupied.

He sat down, breathing very heavily (acting?). 'What are we here for?' he asked.

'Well, one thing is this', I said, handing over the three folders of his bark paintings catalogue. He had asked me to make inquiries on his behalf about its possible publication. I then produced a typed statement, summarising the views of my publisher friend. The material (of course) was excellent, but there was no way it now could be published in black-and-white, as he proposed. I then suggested where he might care to take the project from here. He listened, and accepted this reverse with remarkably good grace.

'There is also another matter', I said, and raised the subject of my inheritance. 'It comes down to this…In the end, either I am your son…or I am not your son. You should leave me a third, or nothing.' I had decided to go for broke.

'It doesn't matter to me any more', he said, wearily.

'Well, it matters to me. There's an estate of probably a million, a million and a half.'

'Rubbish! At the moment I'm struggling to maintain what I've got, with a loan of $290 000!' Always the deflection into the difficulties he was having now – the supreme reality. If things went on like this, there'd be nothing left to inherit.

But I kept up the pressure. He'd helped me financially in the past, he said. When I was under-impressed he accused me of 'scoffing'.

'No, not scoffing. Just stating things that need to be said…I know you don't like my sexuality. But that's not a matter of choice. It was beyond my control: it could have been genetic, a consequence of a late birth, or whatever…'

This he seemed to accept, to brush aside.

'You should take me into the company. Leave me some shares in your will.'

'There are no shares', he said. But whoever heard of a company without shares – however few, or many? He would always bend facts to win an argument. There was no point in pursuing him across this wasteland.

He then explained how the company had been set up to provide for the boys' education.

'Right. That was fair enough. But the situation's now changed. Their education's completed. Hank and Garry are now likely to be much wealthier than I am.'

'How do you know? You haven't got a crystal ball…

Hank could be in hospital tomorrow, incapacitated after an accident on his motor bike!' (The motor bike accident! It was no time to smirk.)

'You should take me into the company', I said. 'Give me an equal share.'

But he didn't see it that way. Hank and Garry had helped to build it up.

'Well', I responded, 'I was never given the opportunity to participate in it. It was set up when I was out of the country. And remember that I have been a good son to you for over forty years — not just over twenty — and have had to bear the weight of your moving from one marriage to another. You've not had to worry about Olga. Meanwhile I've had to accept with good grace the coming into being of this second family, and I've done so — have seen them grow up and assume that pushing me out was perfectly natural. I've loved you, and I've loved my mother; I've also loved Eve, and have listened to you carefully when you've spoken of difficulties in the home. It has taken up a great deal of time, energy…and love.'

I shouldn't have used the word 'love' quite so freely: to Jim it was kryptonite. But he seemed to be moved, a little. As I got up from the table to make the tea he asked, 'How's Olga?'

So — five days before her ninetieth birthday — I gave him a report. Suddenly he said he would leave me one of the flats. It would bring in about $5000 a year.

'Good', I said. 'That would give me some leverage if my job becomes impossible, as it might. And it would enable me to travel', I said, smiling. 'I'm not greedy.'

I now realise that in Jim's view I should have been. (Why didn't I have a family to be greedy for?) I should not have mentioned travel, job: I had exposed myself. Retraction began almost immediately.

He was anxious that the money would be left to 'an outsider' — an old fear of his. Of course wives were not outsiders, they were recruits, their children extending the family tree. I reminded him of the public purpose I then had in mind for my own estate, which he thought a good idea. 'Anyway', I assured him, 'I could, if necessary, sign a contract. There's no problem.'

This he accepted, although as he spoke it became plainer that it was only the *income* from one of the flats that he had in mind. He wouldn't 'harm' the company. It was a private empire, marching under his colours into eternity.

Jim had wanted to have a lunch immediately after — he'd forgotten all about my Canberra meeting. He agreed to have it when I returned, now that things were 'settled'. But when the time came, he was less keen. Months rolled by: for his birthday I gave him a mock Luncheon Voucher (English style), promising 'one lunch in a Superior Restaurant — Superior Company provided'. He didn't get the joke, and I had to explain. What I would have liked to say was, I'm trying to trick you into having lunch with me, you old bastard. But he would have none of it. When I asked him later, over the phone, he simply said, 'It'd be a waste of time'. He had decided to avoid me. Worse, when I rang he increasingly took to general grumbling or making a hostile statement, then hanging up.

BUT ONE DAY HE RANG, AND WAS ABOUT TO GO, WHEN – knowing it would interest him – I mentioned the *Age* that morning carried a report of the death of Ivan Champion. (He was one of the first two white men to walk across New Guinea in 1927–28.) Within five minutes Jim was back on the phone again, asking exactly where it was in the paper. A day or two later came the sequel, in the form of a prominent article.

'Newspaper reports this week that the last of Papua New Guinea's white explorers had died', it began,

> were exaggerated…Mr Davidson himself was among the
> leaders in mapping its mountain ranges and rivers…

> But for a dreadful accident, Mr Davidson might also
> have been the one to uncover the huge wealth of copper
> that is now being mined in the upper reaches of the Ok
> Tedi River.

It was 1939, and because it was 'uncontrolled territory' the explorers had a police escort. Five mornings in a row they had been attacked by headhunters, who ran off when shots were fired in the air. But on the sixth, the tribesmen must have decided the guns were harmless.

'I called out, "Shoot to kill!", and as soon as they saw two or three go down, the others ran off – all except one big bloke who grabbed one of my team…

'I tried to tear him off but he was covered in pig grease. He got up and began to wrestle with me…then we rolled over a precipice. I was underneath and when we hit a rock shelf 10 feet down I stopped while the headhunter kept going the other 200 feet.'

Mr Davidson heard his leg snap…Had it not been a simple fracture, rather than a compound, he would never have survived.

So there it was, up in lights, the tale I had heard elaborated with more and more detail as the years went on. There must have been a stub of truth in it: perhaps a scuffle, a fall, and perhaps a broken ankle. But here it was with an additional wallop of fictions, including the 1934 'air crash' and thirteen years as a coffee planter at Mt Hagen. I was annoyed: by the way he had taken my piece of information and run with it, by the tissue of lies, and the way that he had no awareness that the 'greasy wrestling' (as one of my friends termed it) could appear ridiculous. Was that…your father? people asked. 'Fraid so.

There was also another aspect. With the years, the myth-making had grown: all his life before Melbourne went first, and now the frontier had the additional advantage of eclipsing Olga – and the Forests Commission. In the vacuum South Africa expanded – it gave 'primitive' cred – sometimes to include attending university there. More understandably, when Garry and Hank were small, his second family were always presented as if the entire (nuclear) show.

But this was – beyond its timing – Dadda's last stand. It was in part a statement for those Aboriginal men of high degree in Arnhem Land, now slipping away, the people whom he had come to feel were his true counterparts. The 'greasy wrestling' developed as he felt the need to match the manhood of these veterans. He too had known battle, and in his own way (not least in his own household) was strongly resisting the demands of a rapidly changing world. His sense of himself was now centred on his life as a frontiersman. It was what gave his life its shape, its meaning.

I hadn't yet tumbled to the story's essential falsehood. It now seems a *koikoi*, an endearing little Motu word he always used to make a lie sound like a fib. Olga always spoke of the 1934 (motor bike) accident, never of this one – which, according to the date he now gave, occurred a year after she had married him. It was the accident he would like to have had. Cannibals, rather than cabbages.

SO MUCH FOR MYTH; LIFE WENT ON. SHORTLY AFTER THE greasy wrestling I was unaccountably popular. Once he remarked, in passing, that 'They think they're going to get my money!' Not long after, just twenty minutes after I had turned up at his house, he grabbed his stick and bade me come with him, as he strode into the garden, and then moved beyond. Suddenly he stopped. It was as if he'd changed his mind – or I was the wrong person. But around this time he did give me some money towards the expenses of going to England to give a keynote address at a conference. The title, 'The Manufacture of Australian Culture', seemed to intrigue him; the subject matter, the story of government funding for the arts, interested some- one he was trying to impress, the art collector and author Margaret Carnegie. I wrote and told him how it went; Eve, writing back, said, 'Sounds like you did us proud'.

That he could approve a paper essentially about grants had itself been a surprise. He would normally grumble about them. One exocet phone call was entirely an attack on Bluestone Media, a gay-run business which apparently had received some government support for one of its projects. And once, when visiting, I was standing near his chair as he repeated the cliché of the day: culture should be financed by the trickle-down effect. From *him*. There was nearly a trickle-down effect right then. From *me*.

Apart from one successful hospital visit, my stocks were never so high again. Perhaps he was annoyed that, when he broke with his old accountancy firm, I decided not to follow – as the man I dealt with there was unusually sympatico. Or it may have been annoyance that, in his eagerness to write a book about Aboriginal art, I said I'd help him with it, look over what he'd written, but not help him to actually write it. Secretly he'd already attempted a collaboration with an acquaintance of mine, a woman who was an art historian. It had broken down. I knew that if I got involved in the subject matter there would be too many arguments. And apart from teaching, I had books to write of my own.

It is plainer to me now that while Jim sustained his interest in Aboriginal art, he was finding less joy in it. Once he had got to seventy, it became increasingly impossible for him to venture to his sanctuary in Arnhem Land. Subsequently he became friendly, through being a mentor, with a young woman who was setting out as a dealer in Aboriginal art. He even contrived to come – unannounced – to a book I was launching, since he suspected the dealer, as a friend of the author, would be there. He had little time for me; all I saw, out of the corner of my eye, was a sly smile of lust. They had spoken, Eve told me, nearly every day for two years. And then, once he had opened an exhibition for her, there was nothing. Even though Eve was curdled with jealousy – and thought Jim had allowed himself to be played for a mug – she conceded that Jim had probably found the young woman suddenly a bit uppity, but must have overdone the harsh words. An interview he gave shortly afterwards was full of sourness. There were too many bark paintings being produced, often by young fellas who didn't understand the symbols they were using, the government had got in on the act, the whole scene had become 'bitchy', &c.

Meanwhile I picked up reports – Hank said so, too – that he was always running me down. But I was a bit shocked when, meeting the artist Noel Counihan over dinner, he asked: 'Can't you be nicer to your father?' Not easily. Around this time I was standing near him in his office, when he dropped something. Without a word, he pointed to the object on the floor. Instead of picking it up for him involuntarily, it became an act of submission. 'We run a tight ship here, you know', he once said when I rang and suggested coming to see him. That may have been the time when – getting nowhere with the mantra, 'Either I'm your son, or I'm not' – I ventured, 'You don't really like me, do you? But there it is. I can do nothing about it.' In a whiny voice he protested, 'It's not like that!' It was just that he had to work – was working now...

Given such stonewalling, I found myself reduced to the subtle pleasure of telling him, after I'd returned from a trip to Tasmania, that his old family home on the hilltop now stood empty, open to the elements. His haunting vision had come to pass.

Then there were the halflings. I'd always got on well with Garry – Garry Garrulous. As he retreated into his business and then his marriage, we found something new to draw us together: politics. He was a dyed-in-the-wool Liberal, but our discussions were frank and fair. Susie, his wife, had a warmth brought out by a country upbringing. Garry, after his own fashion, had chosen independence; if it entailed always being listed after Hank, as if the younger of the two, it didn't bother him.

Hank was now on the inside running. He had stronger business instincts, a feeling for the visual and a love of the wilderness that appealed to Jim; he had taken him to Arnhem Land when he was a ten-year-old. Now Hank was company secretary, and after a while Jim let him do the books. He had developed some respect for him, Hank announced one day. Of course, I said; all you need from your father is a bit of trust and confidence.

Our father would not have understood that. He had no conception of loyalty – the idea of two separate intelligences within the family working sympathetically together. What he wanted was obedience, and Hank seemed to give it to him. SJ would ring him at work, at any time, to discuss anything — sometimes three times a day. Hank told how he had devised tactics to avoid these calls; Jim had to be fended off. There were times when he'd wanted to be included in some social activity with Hank and his contemporaries. 'Me! Me! Me!', Hank imitated.

Hank and I got on well at times, but usually there were either strategic silences, or jostling. Once it was me, fumbling, who picked up the phone and nearly dropped it: 'Sorry', I said to the unknown caller. 'I accept your apology', was Hank's response. One day he made a comment directed at me as we all sat together in the lounge: Garry told him to watch it. Much later, I met him and his wife Carly in a restaurant, so as to advise her on how to conduct interviews. I was known there, but Hank was intent on making a big man of himself with the waiters. Then I offered him a ticket to *Faust*. The opera contains both the Devil and a score of good tunes: he sat there entranced. Just before we parted, he thanked me. I said something back; having clambered on to his motor bike, Hank imitated my voice before speeding away. (Thanks, but no obligation.) I bit my tongue.

Meanwhile relations between Dad and Eve were, if anything, worsening. He still resisted her request to sign company cheques, and at his eighty-first birthday Eve was so disgusted with him that she refused to take part in any celebration. Around this time, after he had used threatening language and banged his fist on the table, she decided to give him the same treatment. This took Jim completely by surprise. 'You're mad', he said. 'I live in fear of my life.' This apparent collapse, Eve believed, had its origins in a childhood trauma with his strong-willed mother.

Jim became more paranoid. He took to locking the toolshed (and losing the key), just so Eve couldn't use it – forcing her to buy a spade of her own. He accused her of pinching things, which were invariably found. Eve was now called an 'ignorant slut'.

Some time after, when he went into hospital again, Jim was in such a foul mood that he said that, while he was in there, he didn't want to see her. He complained to me that when he was admitted, he was found to be suffering from malnutrition: 'She just feeds me chops and vegetables every night', he said, 'all because of her bloody painting'. In fact this was a baseless charge: Eve painted only six hours a day, and was at his beck and call even then. The problem was that he'd already made it plain that he wouldn't eat chicken, beef, sausages, veal and other things.

The mounting hostility extended to a retaliatory hacking of each other's favourite plants. Should they be out driving, and Eve challenge him, he could threaten to drive the car into a nearby wall. He had such a perverse sense of honour that there was always the risk he might be mad enough to do it. In the end, Jim's rapidly worsening physical condition may have been the only thing that saved her.

There was a stroke – or something very much like one. Recovery was slow, especially with speech. Once, Eve accompanied Jim into a city building. He walked up to the reception desk and demanded, 'Chairs! Chairs! Where are they?' How could she explain that this is the rudest man in the world – who's had a stroke, and wants to know the way to the lifts…It was tough, for a man who thought of himself as Taubada (Motu for master): that's what he had asked Eve to call him, once he tired of Bukzi. Now he always divided people into 'hostile' and 'friendly', he told me: just like natives. 'It's lonely up there', Eve conceded, and yes, he was a financial whiz. But he had thought of himself as immortal, and now knew he was not. The world was slipping away, he was slipping away, in an entropic end. Once he told me over the phone that he was 'going broke', before launching a tirade against Keating and the Labor government. A lot of it I couldn't understand: it was scrambled, much of it, but the 'bloodys' and the general intemperance came streaming through. If only you could hear yourself, I thought. The delivery matched the parody he was uttering. It was like listening to a Hitler speech on a crackling pre-war radio.

FAMILY CHRISTMAS DINNERS WERE STILL HELD – OCCASIONING a certain dread (I think in us all). On one of these last occasions I was nearly Christmassacred. It began with me waiting for Hank to pick me up. He was quite late, so I rang. Carly answered: she said he was on his way. I tried to have a bit of a chat, but – like an 'efficient' receptionist – she cut me off in mid-sentence, repeating he'd be there shortly.

Over a gin and tonic Hank told me – a development from the vague dissatisfaction with his job he'd indicated earlier – that he was thinking of going out on his own. Interesting…Meanwhile he was unhappy about Christmas. All those presents! It had become a farce. Garry never exerted himself, and just gave him cash to get the presents. We shouldn't have them any more – at least, not ones worth more than ten dollars. I was not happy – this would undercut any demonstration of attachment to the family on my part. You'd better discuss it with Eve, I had said before and repeated now. Christmas is important to her. Then the phone rang: SJ. Where were we? We had both assumed that one o'clock was the time, as usual.

Walking in I placed my presents – wedging a bottle between the feet of a teddy – and looked across to Dad, who smiled. In fact he was affable all day, surprisingly so. He was of course, 'bloody lousy'; that was a given, though no doubt true. Having sorted out that my recent promotion was to Associate Professor – 'Aspro will ease it!' I joked, recalling an old advertising jingle – he congratulated me. Over dinner he asked if I still worked half-time. Yes, I said; it makes for an interesting life, if a more difficult one – journalism, and now some scripts for TV. He even asked about money. I couldn't expect to make much from my books, I said. Which is why I remained at the university, half-time.

By now it was plain that all I would get from Eve were darting looks: she would not return my gaze. The on-going trial of a public figure came up: I suggested that, in view of his philanthropy, he was entitled to some remission. But Eve would have none of it. She argued that, as a leader of society, and therefore as somebody people were inclined to trust, any penalty should be heavier. Soon there was a switch to politics: the forthcoming election. I said I thought Labor wouldn't lose any seats in Victoria. At this Garry shot out his hand. 'I bet you a bottle of Chivas Regal they will!' I accepted, varying the wager to say that I was talking of the total number, rather than particular seats. Accepted. But Eve surged on.

'If anybody votes Labor after ten years of Labor government in Victoria', she said, 'they're stupid'.

'If they'd gone out in '88', I said, 'like they should've, it would have gone down as a good government'.

'Block your ears, Jim!' said Garry. (I pretended to.) 'It was pretty essential that Labor was voted in 1982', he told the table.

'Garry!' I responded – for we had often discussed politics from opposite positions in a friendly fashion – 'There's a rumour going around that you're a generous man. Only

(I looked puzzled)...I can't hear the basis for it.' There was laughter all round.

The present-giving. First up was one of mine for Garry and Susie. Eve squinted at the tag, 'For the builder and his wife'. I explained who it was for. 'We're all builders here!' she declared. It will become clear, I explained. Inside the box was a gingerbread house, and they quite liked it. Eve then opened my 'mini' – a cassette. Harp music. She stared at that for some time, as if I had confused stepmother with mother (not a chance). Then, when she opened the 'major', a book on Grace Cossington Smith, she saw the price I had inadvertently left on – $95. Eve said she had seen it advertised for $65. (Unlikely: she hadn't told me this when we were discussing her gift.) She wanted to pay the balance. No, I said, it doesn't matter; then to mollify her, added, I might just scale down your birthday present a little.

Hank, who had made no fancy, improvised 'minis' this year (didn't get his way over Christmas), simply announced that some money I gave him would go towards his next butch toy. He was sitting next to Dad, who was poring over the pictorial history of Devonport I had given him. Jim kept showing pictures to Hank: 'Right!', Hank would say, as if issuing a receipt. It was as though Hank had given him the book. I was to my father's left, and just a couple of feet away. Despite speaking up, I might just as well not have been there. To my left, as was customary at Christmas, sat Susie, increasingly surrounded by teddy bears. She had expressed a liking for them, and so it became a game. Perhaps she was becoming broody.

It was time to leave. I parted from Jim formally but amiably; a peck for Eve. She decided to trail Hank to his car. On the path the name of an old friend of hers came up, and I showed that I remembered it. Eve listened, decapitating a flower as I spoke. The garden, in fact, looked neglected: because there had been so many disputes, she didn't do any weeding now. Let the eighty-four-year-old do it himself!

We got into the car, and she addressed Hank through the window. 'Thank you for having given up some of your valuable time!' she said, with a sardonic smile. Then, after glowering at me, she moved away.

Revisiting such incidents, I wonder why I showed so much persistence – indeed misplaced persistence. At first I felt it important to have good relations with my father, as a kind of rigorous balance to my indulgent mother. Subsequently, it slowly dawned on me that I was unlikely to have a family of my own: I'd better make the best of the one I had. Then, when in London, my older friend Camo Jackson remarked that at a certain point you decide to stick with people (particularly family) regardless. It was in that spirit that I'd gone to Cromwell Court in 1977, after a two-year break. I would see it out. Beyond any prospects of inheritance, I felt I owed my father loyalty, creating a margin he might one day need to call upon, should there be difficulties with the second family. If necessary, I should make an effort. The trouble was, loyalty was *expected*. Anything else was unconscionable. Father was rather like Lord Milner in South Africa, who on hearing out an address of loyalty from up-country Boers, spat out, 'It'd be damned monstrous if you weren't!', then climbed back into his train and proceeded to the front and the battle with their distant relatives.

There were, too, his spasmodic generosities, and occasionally enjoyable family dinners, even bursts of laughter. Increasingly there had been, and would be until the last phase, a sense of common cause, as Eve and Garry and Hank told me of SJ's latest dramas. My hanging in was also induced partly by a native tenacity, combined with a retro cast of mind: I have always wanted to see the shape of things, preferably in their entirety. I put up with various indignities because I wanted to see how the story would end. That it would end soon – no matter how, now – had become my fervent prayer.

IN THE MIDDLE OF A WINTER'S NIGHT I WOKE UP SUDDENLY and realised I couldn't breathe. I was alone, in a cold dark house. I sat up, but it was no better; got up, it was just the same. Had I somehow been…poisoned? I made my way to the kitchen, thinking there might be a chance I wouldn't come through. Gradually the attack abated. It turned out to be asthma. There were three attacks in a fortnight – one brought on by putting the rubbish bin out at six in the evening. I saw a specialist, who fired more questions at me than anybody else has, before or since: he declared that, at the age of forty-eight, my condition had been 'unmasked'. It seemed tough – in addition to coming out, I had to be unmasked.

Something else was unmasked by this development. None of them rang to ask how I was. Yet ever since returning from overseas, I had visited Dad and Eve once every three weeks. For years there had been a family dinner on these occasions. But now – without a car – I dreaded going out into the cold night air. The pattern of visiting was broken. Eve saw to it that it was never re-established.

This did not come as a complete surprise. On one occasion, at the end of 1981, I was attending a function at a venue nearby, and since I was in the area, thought I'd stroll over. (I was moving to Canberra in a couple of months.) Since I was not expected, I knocked. In the stillness I was eyed by an enormous Sepik guardian spirit figure. When they came to the door, Dad and Eve seemed anything but pleased to see me. It was an upset. 'You're lucky I didn't shoot you', said my father. Thinking I must have just chosen a bad time, I put it out of mind.

Not long after, at a lunch, Hank told me that I should knock at the front door. It was not his right to say so, I said; I never had – when expected – and was not going to start now. He could, if he chose. But this had been my home, before he was born. Dad and Eve were silent; no-one else said anything. Only later I realised that he might have been put up to it.

Unknown to me at the time, there was a deeper intrigue going on. In 1984 Eve was unexpectedly let off the chain – and permitted to go to the Greek island Santorini. Jim must have wanted a change, some time to himself. She went with a friend she had often mentioned. The trip did her a power of good; some time later, Hank mentioned he was house-sitting for a professor of Russian in Canberra. I didn't pay any particular attention. Then one day Eve declared to me that she had met the Christesens. Clem Christesen had been my predecessor at *Meanjin*; his had been the most reluctant retirement in history. No-one had attacked the succession; the real question was whether *Meanjin* should be allowed to continue. But the Christesens' grievance against me was deep, and ineradicable. Eve's friend apparently knew them, and must have mentioned her, and her surname; whereupon I suspect it was Nina Christesen (who held an academic post in Russian) who showed most interest in meeting. Whatever the case, it seems likely that she played on Eve's stepmotherly feelings, endorsing them. (She was a great hater.)

Eve now stood at the kitchen door and told of their meeting(s) as if this was the most normal thing in the world: Clem this, Nina that…'That's what I call them', she said. I was gobsmacked. You're consorting with my enemies, I wanted to say. But didn't, for I had to tread carefully, since this news was tantamount to a declaration of hostility. I was shocked – all the more so because Eve had chosen an indirect, almost acceptable way of declaring it. On a number of levels, their socialising was unbelievable. If I asked questions, or commented, who knew what can of worms would be opened? I needed to hold firm if I were to remain a player right to the end.

A month or so after my asthma attacks, Olga died. 'Go on!' Jim said, when I told him over the phone. He had asked to be present at Olga's funeral, and mentioned it a couple of times – to provide support for me, he said. I preferred not to have it, and was glad that Father's Day provided the right interval for ringing him after Olga had been buried. Had Jim attended, he would have assumed his default position of dominance: jingling money in his pocket, and at an inappropriate moment saying, 'Let's go, Jim!' I felt it would have been a betrayal of her. She wouldn't have escaped him even in death. Although I sent him a copy of my tribute, along with a printed card, I knew he was not pleased. Not that it mattered much. He didn't even inquire about the will, which surprised me. Perhaps he imagined she was as poor as he left her. The inheritance was not large, but it was useful. I decided not to tell him. It was a severance: the first time I had withheld any serious financial information.

Perhaps a prompt had been the way Eve had responded when I said my term on an Australian Research Council committee was coming to an end. She couldn't see why it could not be extended, probably imagining it to be a bigger thing than it was – since she had little experience of public life. She was always very firm about what she knew, but instead of being aware of its limitations, became judgemental instead. For her, this was another case of my financial delinquency – like not having a full-time job. Taking that view relieved her of any necessity to consider that I might have a legitimate claim on the estate.

I had begun to see that loyalty, unappreciated, was a kind of masochism. Putting a sweet face on abusive behaviour was just icing the shitcake. Worse, it set one up for victimhood, inducing a sense of fatalism. This was serious, in one with a temperament attuned to the past: I could develop a taste for the subtler hues of relegation. I became determined to resist – stand my ground – although (if I could manage it) not to the point of open defiance.

In the meantime there had been a further moving away by my father. One day, not long after I had told him of Olga's death, I found a message from him on the answering machine. I returned the call. After a halting beginning, he announced: 'So there won't be any argument, I've decided to give you a sum of money, now.'

'Oh yes… How much?'

'Ten thousand dollars. I'll arrange with the accountants to get the sum paid immediately!'

'Ten thousand dollars? But that's less than the five thousand a year we discussed before.'

'This cuts right across that.'

Pause. 'I'm afraid that's unacceptable.'

'Look. Half my factories are empty. There are plenty of ways I can use ten thousand dollars, I'm telling you.'

I figured that at the very least I would get that much from the others. And deny him satisfaction. 'OK', I said, followed by his curt goodbye.

Not long after, a letter arrived acknowledging Olga's memorial card. It was focused on the $10 000, and the property that was to have provided me with some income. That had to be sold, he said; it had been vacant for two months, and was disposed of along with other things. In his mind, getting rid of the property served to cancel the commitment. As for the broader principle of succession, he had dispensed with that already. Instead, this stricken elderly man implicitly appealed for pity, signing off as follows: 'From you battered old Dad and bloodies at last.' But stocks of sympathy for him had long been exhausted. A written call for it, though, was something new – but I would have been despised if I'd shown any. Later it turned out to have been a cover for another hostile act. These were the black tears of a squid.

Before I set off on a three-week research trip to

England, Jim had been pleasant to me. But on my return he showed his irritation a number of times. The phone was again the weapon of choice, delivering rudeness when least expected. We were having a late celebration of his birthday, and once again he had been rude. When I said I'd been to St Paul's Cathedral, he said, 'Don't tell me you've gone all religious.'

'No', I replied. 'I just went there to pray for your soul.'

My blood was up. Giving him a book on safaris, I added that some of the pictures were in black-and-white. Perhaps he could colour them in, putting himself in the picture. He was puzzled, so I said that if you were rude to people you must expect some sharpness back. I urged the others to support me, particularly Susie, who was sitting nearest. But she moved awkwardly, refused with a little negative nod to say anything, while the others were silent as stones. Jim said nothing either, just sat there looking amazingly blank-faced, apart from a slight sardonic smile: I had revealed my true colours. Any infraction, or lapse, was always regarded as the ultimate indicator of attitude. (As with natives, so with offspring.) So far as he could effect it, I would be shot at dawn.

At a dinner some time before, Hank had shouted across a table in a noisy restaurant, 'You own your own house?' (Not yet.) It seemed an odd question to ask, under those circumstances. I didn't pay much attention at the time; but when they came to my house for the following midwinter dinner they seemed to be noisier than usual – so it seemed from my listening post in the kitchen. And that year the wonderful birthday cards Eve used to make for me abruptly ceased.

I knew something had happened, not long after, when a friend in the art world told me that she had come across them dining in the Cafe Latin. It was another appropriated haunt of mine: once, when we entered it together, one waiter said to another, 'Padre e figlio' (father and son). For the irony was that I was the son who looked most like him: Garry and Hank used to joke that one of them was the son of the milkman, the other of the postman. But they were there that night to celebrate – so I learned from another source – the putting of his affairs in order. My art world friend was the spectre at the feast. She told him how she had been a student of mine, had learned much, sang my praises. 'I'm glad I've got three sons', said my father tightly.

What they did not know was that, with the help of a lawyer friend, I had been monitoring developments and knew that in 1991 my father had finally abdicated, formally relaxing his control of the company. He remained a director, but was no longer a shareholder. I had, of course, not been told. There had never been a row: I had given no pretext for a formal expulsion. I had just been quietly done away with. That process had begun with the formation of the company, nearly twenty years earlier. I had hoped that by participating as fully as I could in family life, a complete overriding of my interests would become unthinkable, seem unjust. Wrong. The family geometry was against me. So now at family occasions, as they tried to shake me off, there was a certain grim satisfaction in seeing just how far they were prepared to go. I had nothing more to lose; and being caught up in a narrative that was not of my devising, I wanted to see how it would end – from the inside.

JIM WAS IN HOSPITAL AGAIN: THE REPAT, HEIDELBERG. WHEN I went to see him, he had his back to me as I entered the room, then rolled over with a huge smile. It vanished immediately. *I'll take that grin off your face...*I wasn't Hank. 'I told them only to let in family', he snarled.

'You forget that I, too, am family', I said, sitting down.

'Your're here, aren't you? So what are you bawling about?' The words spat out.

He then turned away, snuggling into the bedclothes. Soon I asked him whether he'd like to be left to sleep. There wasn't much point in staying. Back to the train and tram.

On another occasion he did feel in the mood, and there was a good conversation. I had brought some old postcards of the North-West Coast, some of which he must have seen when young. They brought back memories, knowledges – he even pointed out different kinds of bullocks, and what they were called. As he spoke, softly – perhaps partly induced by his condition – a trace of an earlier accent also reappeared. He sounded like an old bushie. But in there was still the sharp fear of losing control: the past had a tug. He brought the viewing to an abrupt end.

Much later, after a further period in hospital, he was surprised when once I said that I'd tried to see him. Did they deliberately keep us apart? Was he told that I showed no interest in coming to see him?

Meanwhile, having a conversation with a student next-door neighbour, it turned out that she had picked up a part-time job in Ravenswood. In Ravenswood? Whereabouts...? Soon she divulged she was working at Cromwell Court, for Dad and Eve. It was the first I'd heard of it. They asked about me from time to time, she said.

The cold war, as I now took it to be, continued. When occasionally I rang to say that I would like to visit them at Cromwell Court, Eve always made out there were difficulties. Once she said she was busy. Inquiries about my father's health, when he was in hospital, were treated brusquely. The last time I paid a visit on my own, she kept me on a short lease, 'managed' me – as though, in a dramatic turning of the tables, Jim was now her prisoner, receiving a formal visitor.

There was a repulsive scrupulousness in giving me

what was mine in the year or two before he died. It was a separation, I realised at the time, so that I would have no claim on them whatsoever. Once I was talking to Jim as he lay on his bed, when suddenly he indicated a particular book that I'd lent him on South Africa. I handed it over, and he handed it back. I let out a gasp – he'd had it for thirty years, and had known all this time it was mine. But now it was de-acquisitioned: he wanted the break to be clean. At the last family dinner he attended at my place, he brought a parcel as a present, neatly killing two birds with one stone. It turned out to consist entirely of juvenilia by me. Similarly Eve brought over a couple of cartons of classic comics and popular history magazines that I'd long forgotten about. Here they now were: tattered from heavy use. 'Go for it!' she said. No, she wouldn't stay. She was just the delivery woman.

There were still the family observances. Once Jim came into the kitchen just after I arrived: I had begun talking to Eve and Hank, who were sitting nearby. Now Jim held the floor, his left arm adjacent to me. From where I was sitting, I slipped a couple of fingers into his curled hand. As he talked on, they were taken – under Hank's watchful eye. It had been a gamble, but I was counting on Dadda seeing himself as the great generative being. Hank's response was to propose that he and Carly – a rarity for them – put on a family dinner, in July. That effectively gazumped my midwinter occasion.

For one of Jim's last birthdays, Garry had put some early home movies on to DVDs. Susie began to laugh loudly: she kept it up for twenty minutes. Deference to Dadda had become a state religion. (Eve on Susie: 'She really fits in'.) The place certainly needed something, even if forced laughter. There was a grimness about it, a chill: silence, sullenness, no music. Passing through the pantry with all that tinned food it felt like an old fortress, waiting for some external threat that never came.

WOULD THIS BE THE LAST CHRISTMAS? CARLY IN THE CAR, already practising a vacuous smile. She wore it round the garden, as Jim showed her over it. I was left to follow behind, or go hang myself; in fact I stumbled upon them. For no sooner had I crossed the threshold than Hank was extracted by Himself; together they went into the main bedroom, firmly closing the door as they got up to financial tricks together. I went through to the kitchen. Eve announced that she and Susie were having a private conversation, while they were preparing the dinner. There was no sign of Garry. And so, after a time, I had gone into the garden.

When we advanced upon the table, I noticed there were place cards: 'Jim – Dad', said one nervously; 'Jim Jr.' said mine, a formulation I have always hated. Usually I sat at his right hand; this time I was well away. That,

Eve explained, was so he could be seated next to his daughters-in-law, and kept occupied that way. Still, I was next to Garry. 'I wonder how big my helping will be today?' he said, aware of the usual index of favour. (His portion could have been reduced, for lateness). Garry and I chatted on: no politics this time, which was unusual. I mentioned I was off to South Africa, to write an article. 'Oh yeah', said the old man, with complete indifference.

Soon it was present time. On the tags, no 'love' from Hank and Carly, although everyone else got their ration. And I noticed that Eve simply handed over my presents, rather than saying – as she did with the others – who they were from. So he opened the wrapping to a bottle of Noilly Prat and, turning to Hank on his right, asked who it was from.

'From Jim', said Hank.

'Who?'

'From Jim', Hank repeated.

'From who?'

'Yesss!!! From Jim!' I shouted across the room. 'Your eldest son… Remember?'

Silence from them all, as they sat like statues of Rameses.

I was thanked.

Shortly after my father was presented with another gift. In his hands, a book. Not the one he had hoped to write on bark paintings, but the one that had been so long coming from his son. It was one of the two advance copies of *Lyrebird Rising*. He sat turning its pages in rapt absorption, seeking out the pictures, and carefully reading the biog. note on the son he had made a stranger. When he had finished, he looked up. I nodded; he nodded in return. The others joined in praise of it too, to their credit.

It was time to go. Hank announced that he and Carly were driving straight to Yarrawonga — then added, after a pause, via my suburb. A little joke: taxis are impossible on Christmas Day.

I shook my father by the hand: he couldn't quite look me in the eye. A pyrrhic victory? I picked up my presents, which I'd put down. 'It's like going through customs', I said, which drew a smile.

Four or five days later there were some early photographs — of my childhood and Tasmania — in the mail, with a short note. Yes, he was giving me what he conceded to be mine — now — so that his heirs need have nothing to do with me.

ONE NIGHT IN OCTOBER 1994 THE PHONE RANG. GARRY. SJ had died. Oh. I hadn't been called to the bedside: was just being informed now. At least the most agreeable member of the family had been delegated to do the job.

'So what's being done?' I asked. He was ringing to discuss a time for the funeral. 'I go to South Africa on Sunday; it's a difficult time'.

'Of course!' said Garry.

It was set for the Friday. That would be difficult, too. An unseasonal high-temperature day promised to irradiate a public transport strike. A fleet of taxis would have to be ordered, to get me through it. The day would be a bizarre one: it began with a hostile interview for promotion at my workplace (I couldn't postpone it), and would culminate in a literary dinner, and the award of a prize for *Lyrebird Rising*. ('Thank you for the cheque, Mr Premier', I said to Jeff Kennett. 'So much better than a Chinese burn.')

The funeral drew forty or fifty, most of them unknown to me. He did have magnetism. The officiating clergyman cleverly hinted that he was a difficult man; an RSL man also spoke, and the *Last Post* was played. The coffin, as was the prerogative of returned men, was covered by the Australian flag – to which Jim had shown no particular attachment during his lifetime. The clergyman correctly listed me as first among the children. Hank had made all the arrangements; Carly – alone – was ostentatiously weeping. When it was time for the body to be removed, Jim was not carried out by his three sons, and one other. Hank had said there would be no pall-bearers: recognition of my connection was avoided. And so he departed the chapel on a squeaky trolley – not to squeals from grandchildren running about. Later, the Fijian farewell song was played: Hank fished for a compliment, which I readily gave. Jim always said he would see black angels...although he didn't quite mean fuzzy-wuzzy ones. Despite everything, he was not unaware of the wrongs he had done.

An old tenant from Monash Avenue was present, and it was the day I met his former lover Claire Lines. People were friendly; it was plain that on Christmas cards he had kept parading my occasional achievements. But Eve was very firm in talking to me, almost bossy. Later, Carly came up; as I turned to greet her, I was aware of a sound…and yes, she was hissing at me. I couldn't believe it. Shortly afterwards Susie came over. We talked, and then suddenly she gave me a full kiss on the lips. It seemed like the Kiss of Peace, the blessing in dismissal of the heretic about to be burnt at the stake. I'd had enough already that day. I wiped it away with the back of my hand.

I asked where the wake was, and was told by Eve there was none. (Years later, I discovered that was a lie.) In taking my leave, I said, I expect I'll hear from you, and we'd get in touch when I came back from South Africa. She agreed. But when I returned three weeks later, there was nothing. A week later a copy of the will arrived from the lawyers. It had been drawn up twelve months earlier, just before the Christmas my father pretended not to hear my name. There were two items that affected me. One was the bequest of a Trobriand Islands table, which I had requested – since I could remember when I was no higher, standing next to it. This was now hollowed out, as it would be transferred to me only on the (permanent) closure of his gallery. The second item was a legacy of $10 000. My father felt 'under no obligation' to make any greater provision, as his son 'has not made any effort to fit into my family life'. And so he exited, telling one of his biggest whoppers.

I did not ask, nor was I told, how they had arranged the disposal of his remains.

I wrote to Eve, as the matriarch. I set aside my relations with my father, and concentrated on my relations with the rest of them, and how I had been a good family member. I said I had always recognised that by far the greatest part of the estate would go to the second family. That was not the issue. But the arbitrary elimination of income from one of the flats, and its replacement by an offer of a single payment of $10 000, was unjust. (And was obscurely connected with Olga's death.) I therefore proposed that the equivalent of the income from that flat for twenty years be turned into a payment of $100 000. As the assets my father had built up would have been worth the best part of two million (exempting the house), this was scarcely an outrageous claim. The single payment would enable an honourable parting of the ways.

'I appreciate that you would like the will to be different', came the reply, written with a certain relish in big, black letters. 'I am unwilling, and unable, to change it.' I was not fully aware, then, that she had form. Eve had quarrelled – and broken – with her sister over inheritance matters. Then I tried to see Hank: he just referred me to his lawyers.

Did they have no empathy? We had all suffered at his hands. At one of the last gatherings Eve had shocked me when, seated in the lounge, she said, 'Let's face it, SJ is a cunt. He's a cunt.' But no-one oppresses like the recently oppressed: the Korean guard syndrome of the Second World War. Apart from the tug of greed, they saw me as connected with them only through *him*. Eventually Eve proposed to pay me another $10 000 – in stages.

Yet Eve had been reminded that, from London years before, I had written at a difficult moment to say that, should Jim die suddenly, when it came to Hank and Garry, I would help financially. And she had, in the early days of the marriage, indicated that she would, for estate purposes, regard me as a son along with her own. But it was different now: the boot was on the other foot, and I would be kicked. Once, when Garry was talking solidly about the company as I was leaving, I asked her about my share of the estate. 'Everybody will get their share!' she declared, her hand resting on the front door. She had acquired a facility for lying. On one of the last visits – in response to her litany of complaint – I said that I had gradually come to see that my father was my worst enemy. She gave me a very strange look. I thought then that she would probably tell him (and she may have done). But what she knew, and I didn't, was that she could run him a very close second.

Hers had been a *via dolorosa*, a way paved with tears. After Eve's initial exhilaration in the marriage – as it opened out a number of horizons simultaneously – there had slowly come a realisation about the nature of the man she had partnered with. Then followed a long period when she felt confined, and became depressed. Eventually, encouraged by Hank's presence, she began a phase of resistance, and, in Jim's last years, began to emerge as a matriarch. Ironically, she would become one of those enduring women Jim most admired. As a compensation for all she had endured, what my father had seen as his wealth became for her the property of the family. By her definition, that family excluded me. And in practical terms, I was marginal to the family, the business, the Arnhem Land outrigger. It was not that there had been any row. Nor that Eve, or any of them apart from my father, were homophobic. I had simply been in the way.

Early in December the phone rang. Eve: 'It's that time of the year again'. I was being invited to Christmas dinner! Incredible…She told me how Hank was busying himself getting rid of some of SJ's stuff, as though I was an acquaintance who did not have any direct involvement. It was an amicable conversation, but no. Almost immediately I felt it would result in a hiding on the way to nothing. There was too much entrenched hostility from all but Garry and Susie. The second family had commodified itself impregnably as 'the company', administering a trust. As Victorian law was then constituted, I could do little about it. Nor did I particularly want to. I was fifty-two: my father had taken up more than enough of my life, and I wanted to be shook of him. He had gutted his assets, transferring practically everything to the rest of his family. It has become plainer to me, in writing this book, that he was of unsound mind. But that would have been hard to establish in a court of law, and would have availed me little.

So I wrote a letter declining the invitation, saying that I hoped that one day matters might be settled satisfactorily, and I could join them at Christmas dinner once again. Apart from the delayed payment, I have not seen or heard from them from that day to this.

IV

In tranquillity

Friends are God's apology for relatives.

Hugh Kingsmill

THE ASMATI OF PAPUA NEW GUINEA TRADITIONALLY sleep on their fathers' skulls, as a means of drawing strength from their ancestors. Metaphorically in this book I have done this; I thank him for this dreaming.

The present is another country. They do things differently here. There have been the technological changes – unparalleled since the Industrial Revolution – together with a new modishness for change and disruption. Beyond that, whoever would have thought St Petersburg would suddenly reappear on the map of Europe? Or that we would live to see the withering away of the state...under capitalism? It is not surprising that even in distant Arnhem Land some bark painters have taken to black-and-white, their totemic backgrounds rendered loosely – as if about to be swept away in the vortex of postmodernism.

And in sexual matters, despite a strong rearguard action, there has been an extraordinary change in attitudes. The polls show a steadily increasing support for marriage equality. And recently, a Victorian minister ordered his department to investigate 'the extent of any underground activity...and see what can be done to minimise the damage caused by these abhorrent practices'. He was not referring to gays. No, the target of these remarks were the religious zealots who want to straighten them out. In Parliament, instead of an occasional cloaked reference to someone's suspect sexuality, it is now possible for one leading politician to denounce another as a homophobe. Meanwhile the old binary has come to be replaced by a smorgasbord of sexualities. The list threatens to become as long as the Catalogue Aria in *Don Giovanni*: LGBTIQ…

If you live long enough, you'll see everything.

I AM ONE OF THE LAST BRITISH-AUSTRALIANS – AS A hyphenated condition. I was born a few months after the fall of Singapore in 1942. In retrospect, this became the most crucial British defeat of the twentieth century. But in Australia British Australia kept on keeping on, running on empty. 'There is a tendency', said the Liberal Arthur Fadden in 1947, 'to forget that we were British'. Labor leaders had made similar statements. It is not surprising, then, that many of us were still educated on outdated assumptions – something which spread far beyond the private schools.

The decline of that world has been spectacularly swift. China, a country that in my boyhood was regarded (beyond Communism) as being backward, two years ago sent its leader on a state visit to the UK. Now England is the decaying, intricate civilisation, addicted to arcane rituals, with China technoid and rising.

Sometimes the British Empire is referred to as though it were entirely an external agency, something acting on Australia, rather than an entity with which Australians were loosely integrated. 'Australia' did not come about by virgin birth; it shared in being British more than it realised. 'Mates in the Empire', as Donald Horne memorably termed it; a mateship that involved soldiering – overwhelmingly by volunteers. My father, amongst other things, provides an interesting case study of how much the old Australia was bound up in the Empire project. As the English writer and politician Tristram Hunt saw it, Melbourne goes on inhabiting its imperial past, but, with a kind of 'historical amnesia', never acknowledges it.

Yet it is there – and sometimes brought home dramatically. A couple of years ago the State Library of Victoria was having a facelift. Out front, a Victorian worthy stood imperturbably on his pedestal, gazing into the beyond; native grass (temporarily) was rising up around him. Two Muslim women, veiled and as black as shadows, glided one behind the other up the shallow steps. They were heading towards the colonnade, half-covered in drop cloths, leaving four massive columns exposed. I blinked in the sun: was this the past, or was this the future? Had we/ would we become Baalbek?

Colonialist assumptions remain in Australia largely undisturbed. Put simply, because the conquest of Australia was so complete, its very nature has been obscured. In South Africa, at the height of apartheid, it was rarely possible for whites to go about their daily business and not encounter a black person within an hour or two. Not so here. Instead, there was the myth that the place was empty – not taken – and that there was 'wealth for all'. In fact, white Australia waxed fat on a seized country. It might even be said that while we have been 'de-dominionised' (gradually working through to a separate identity from Britain), the Aborigines are yet to be fully decolonised.

In South Africa, once there was majority rule, reconciliation was followed by transformation. Sometimes this was drastic: blacks moved into the best jobs, white beggars began to appear on the streets. The challenge in Australia is infinitely less. But here reconciliation is often seen not as a beginning, but as a symbolic statement disjunctive from all else. As was shown by the shameful booing of Adam Goodes, the attitude seems to be that Aboriginal people should be *grateful* that we have reconciled with them. We have a long way to go. It may yet be the case that Australia, 'settled' as South Africa was, may have to undergo a similar process of dismantling or radically transforming the settler state. It will just be slower – unless there are external pressures – more extended in time.

Imperial dominance rested on patriarchy – was almost its outward projection. This book has been an exploration of one telling example of that nexus. And, to some extent, a reverse proposition has also been true. Feminism as a political movement may have emerged at the height of imperialism; but its more potent second wave got into its stride with the dissolution of the Empire. In my own case, in relation to Australia, I once proposed to bring together various writings on the theme of de-dominionisation, exploring Australia's slow growth to political and cultural maturity. That I should be sensitive to this issue is no accident. The proposed title for that book would have done almost as well for this one: *Getting Out from Under*.

For Jim became an anachronism, an unbending projection of the past. His idea of indigenous people had been engendered by family experience of Africa, the romances of Rider Haggard, and his own quest for the exotic in the Islands. (Arnhem Land was an autumn romance.) Everything was firm, unequivocal, and placed him at the centre of events, which he felt enabled and entitled to control. The contest with various opponents was the thing; his women and children were just auxiliaries. Livestock. And, as the great liberal project weakened, with socialism dying and the old humane culture becoming more and more marginalised, he achieved a remarkable thing: with his talent for business matters, he leapt from the world of Umslopogaas to that of Milton Friedman. For Jim, as for Margaret Thatcher, there was no such thing as society: only family, and 'contacts'. But as this story shows, for his wives and children it came at a terrible cost.

With me there need not have been a damaging rupture. There's the instructive case of Ian Smith, the leader of white Rhodesia. His one son led a wild life – liquor, drugs, the counter-cultural style. In 1972, Alec Smith heard a voice on the car radio telling him to go home and read the Bible. He did – and was a changed man. Still a rebel, he became converted to the cause of majority rule. The black leaders – no doubt suspicious at first – befriended him, and soon he became a covert channel of communications between his father's government and the nationalists. By the end of the decade, Ian Smith was defeated and Zimbabwe was born. But in his final years, the father and son became very close.

In fact I tried to remember the good things about Jim, and set aside a particular day to do so: 16 December, the old Dingaan's Day of white South Africa. But it was a failure: it was fated to be under-nourished. Instead, I noticed a few years after he died that my sudden depressions had lifted. The more I thought about it, the more the Mackenzies in Tasmania had been my true family – apart from another I have been welcomed into in middle age. As for Olga, since the day she died in 1990 was also her ninety-second birthday, I decided almost immediately that I would always visit her grave on that day, and on no other.

Jim would find it very difficult to disinherit me now in the manner he chose. Family trusts are not as inviolable as once they were, in the case of unjust omissions. Other jurisdictions have traditionally handled these matters much better. In Scotland, for example, it is simply impossible to disinherit any child absolutely. Sensibly, since there may be domestic complications, the house can be left to whomever the testator determines. But when it comes to moveable property, one half invariably goes to the children, as the 'legitim' or bairns' portion.

THE YEARS ROLLED ON. PEOPLE WOULD ASK ABOUT FAMILY. Occasionally I would tell them, but often they didn't like what they heard. 'That's a terrible thing to say about your father', said one woman at a dinner party. 'No', I corrected, 'it's a terrible thing to *have* to say about your father'. Sometimes I'd bat with a flippancy. Now that I'm in a time belt where families are often in ruins, the question shifts, casting away the complications. 'Do you have any children?' people ask. How else could I respond, except to smile sweetly and say, I am my own child.

But sometimes I play a more elaborate game. If you don't have a family, it may be necessary to invent one. So there's my wife Barbara, who sadly died twelve years ago with breast cancer, and our two children, Evelyn and Michael. Evelyn is thirty-nine, and a hospital administrator; she's married to Rick, who's a schoolteacher (maths): they have two children, Roland, doing well at Trinity Grammar and shaping up to do law, and Vicky, who's fifteen. My son, Michael, thirty-seven, lives in Sydney and is an architect. If all this seems to be going over well, drawing intelligent responses, I then go for broke. Michael is GAY, and living with his partner, Steve (in IT)…

I had always hoped for some sort of reconciliation with Garry and Hank, and suddenly realised that time was running out. I would shortly be seventy; Garry was approaching his fiftieth birthday. That surely must be the occasion – any other would come too late. But they had cut me off, unrepentantly: to extend the olive branch was generosity enough. I could not go more than half way. Remembering Garry's old interest in ships, I sent a post-card of a large passenger liner docked at Circular Quay. On the back I wrote a short message, indicating that I had not forgotten his birthday, and conveying my best wishes for the day and the years ahead.

I then realised, with horror, that I had miscalculated. In my eagerness to send the card, I had muddled up the weekend on which it fell, and so sent it early. Well, I thought, at least I did it. And just possibly…I could now be included in the celebrations. That did not happen. Nothing did. There was no response whatsoever.

It got worse. Some three weeks later, the *Age* contained a large box death notice. For Eve, who had died at home. She had already been buried – for, in the contemporary fashion, even funerals are privatised. Private funerals always privilege the recent. Somebody may have played a crucial role in another's life a long time ago, that has not been forgotten by that person; the opportunity to pay respects, to learn more about the deceased, is simply denied. But here there was malice. The last thing the second family wanted at that funeral was me turning up.

There was more. In the death notice there was mention of four grandchildren. These were relatives I did not even know I had. That hurt.

I now realised that, apart from being passed over in the Company, I had been unpersoned. As far as the family was concerned, I did not exist. The injustice of it rankled.

But within a few weeks I came to see that they had done me a service. They had provided closure to the story of my father, a narrative which had begun in Ladybrand a full century before. Perhaps I should write it: historians are, after all, 'professional remembrancers', as Eric Hobsbawm put it, 'of what their fellow citizens wish to forget'.

And so I began this book. In the act of thinking and writing, the more immediate prompts were soon overtaken by other imperatives. It became an exercise in achieving understanding: of my father, of families, and even the wider context of the values and experiences associated with the late British Empire. How they had affected him, and how they affected me.

Everybody makes the best of the hand they have been dealt, but it is as if one vital card is missing. So I have come to accept the duplicity of Eve, and the compliance of Hank and Garry. But my father's ruthlessness is something else. I suspect he rather fancied a book being written about him; the devil would be in the detail. Well, here it is…Not quite the book he wanted.